THE
MAKING OF AMERICA
SERIES

ELIZABETH
THE FIRST CAPITAL
OF NEW JERSEY

Trolley cars run down the center of First Street in this undated photograph of Elizabeth. A horse and wagon are parked at the curb on the left.

THE
MAKING OF AMERICA
SERIES

ELIZABETH
THE FIRST CAPITAL
OF NEW JERSEY

JEAN-RAE TURNER AND
RICHARD T. KOLES

ARCADIA

Published by Arcadia Publishing,
an imprint of Tempus Publishing, Inc.
2 Cumberland Street
Charleston, SC 29401

For all general information contact Arcadia Publishing at:
Telephone 843-853-2070
Fax 843-853-0044
E-Mail sales@arcadiapublishing.com

For customer service and orders:
Toll-Free 1-888-313-2665

Visit us on the Internet at http://www.arcadiapublishing.com

Front cover: *This is a 1923 aerial photograph of the Union County Courthouse and the First Presbyterian Church on Broad Street. The Courthouse faces Elizabeth Avenue, and the jail is in the foreground. The church graveyard is to the left, and the training ground is the grassy spot in front of all three.*

CONTENTS

ACKNOWLEDGMENTS

Between us we covered the Elizabeth area for more than 50 years as a reporter and photographer for the *Elizabeth Daily Journal*. Many of these photographs illustrated our stories and much of the information contained in this book was acquired during these assignments and updated for this project. We are grateful to the many people who assisted us. They are numerous.

Among them are Robert Bacbanell and Charles Bool of the Elizabeth Public Library, Walter E. Boright, John Brennan, Reverend Howard Bryant, Peter Campbell, Betty Lou Crawley, Frank J. Cicarell, Donald Schissl, Patrick Di Fulio, Kathleen Dunn, Sister Jacinta Fernandes, Edward I. "Buzzy" Fox, Robert Fridlington, Bill and Ruth Frolich, Warren Grover, Douglas Harris, Kenneth Hobson, James Jandrowitz, Reverend Father William Kelly, Bernice Kessler, Linda Lee Kelly, Robert M. Kirkland, Raymond Lehnes, Stephanie Laucius, Daniel Maynard, Richard Mushko, Robert O'Leary, Earl Olinger, Gene Picker, Elwood Pryor, Reverend James L. Reisner, Steve Rinaldi, Chief Lester Sargent, Charles Shallcross Jr., Freeholder Daniel P. Sullivan, John Surmay, Rabbi Elazar Teitz, Richard P. Thompson, Angela Tomklewicz, E. Jane Townsend, Howard Wiseman, Michael Yesenko and the Sisters of the Benedictie Motherhouse, and the Office of Mayor J. Christian Bollwage.

Special thanks to Donald L. Davidson, proprietor of New Jersey Newsphotos from 1964 to 1999, for permitting us to use some photos from his collection; and to Barbara Moss and Darren and Lauren Yeats for assisting us with the mysteries of the computer.

INTRODUCTION

Elizabeth was the first English-speaking settlement in New Jersey. Dutch fur traders occupied the Hudson and Raritan River Valleys, while Finns and Swedes settled along the lower Delaware River. Colonel Richard Nicolls sailed into New Amsterdam and captured it quickly for the British crown in October 1664. He gave the colonists from the eastern end of Long Island, known as the Associates, the right to settle in the future New Jersey. Colonel Nicolls's governorship lasted less than a year. On August 1, 1665, Captain Philip Carteret arrived with 30 persons aboard the *Philip*. He named the settlement Elizabethtown for his cousin, Lady Elizabeth Carteret, and the new colony New Jersey for his homeland, the Isle of Jersey, one of the English Channel Islands.

The area was given to the Duke of York, the future King James II of England, by his brother King Charles II. The duke, who was in debt, immediately gave the land to Sir George Carteret, Elizabeth's husband, and John Lord Berkeley, to whom he owed money. The Concessions and Agreements granted the colonists by Governor Nicolls promised the settlers their rights as Englishmen and religious freedom. Religious freedom was rare in the seventeenth century. They also were required to pay quitrents including peppercorn, a black berry, in five years for the land. The demand became one of the grievances for the Revolutionary War.

By the time of the American Revolution, Elizabethtown was the largest hamlet in New Jersey with an estimated population of 1,200 people, prosperous farms, gifted craftsmen, intelligent lawyers, and flourishing businesses. Elizabethtown, with its ferry service to New York City, served as the gateway to New Jersey and Philadelphia, the colonies' largest settlement. Stagecoach lines and later railroads traveled through it carrying people to all points in the new nation.

During the Revolutionary War, Elizabethtown was under attack for eight long years. A resident never knew from day to day if his home, horses or cows, fences or sheds, fine furniture, or silver and other belongings would still be there. It was the only war in the nation's history in which the city was entered and occupied by enemy troops.

After the war there was an intensive period of recovery, rebuilding, replanting, and restoration. Elizabethtown began to enter the industrial revolution as craftsmen disappeared and machines took their place. By 1855, the hamlet was ready to become the City of Elizabeth. Various arguments with its neighbor Newark resulted in divorcing Essex County and becoming the seat of Union County, New Jersey's youngest and second smallest county in 1857.

The years after the Civil War showed much promise for Elizabeth. Residents could travel to the New Jersey shore, New York City, Philadelphia, or the West on the railroads. The Singer Sewing Machine Company built a huge factory on Newark Bay. The City Council made improvements such as water mains with fresh water, storm and sanitary sewers, and paved streets. Large Victorian-style residences fronted on tree-lined streets. The panic of 1873 plunged the nation into a five-year depression and Elizabeth, unable to pay its debts for improvements, declared bankruptcy in 1879. It took until 1922 to pay back all of the debts.

Other nationally known companies such as American Type Foundry and Simmons Mattress Company moved into the city. From the early 1890s until 1920, ships were built along the Arthur Kill. Electric trolleys, diners, and automobiles were manufactured. The city sent its best and bravest young people to serve in World Wars I and II. New roads to the countryside encouraged young people returning from the wars to marry and start their own families. Factories unable or unwilling to change for the twenty-first century died.

Today Elizabeth continues to be a gateway to the world. U.S. Highways 1 and 9, Routes 24, 27, and 28, and the New Jersey Turnpike traverse the city. Half of the Newark-Elizabeth seaport and the Newark Liberty International Airport are in Elizabeth. Routes 21, 22, and 78; the Garden State Parkway; the New York Throughway; and Routes 80 and 280 are a short distance away. The New Jersey Transit trains have replaced the stagecoach lines and ferry boats.

While the huge industries are gone, hundreds of smaller ones have taken their places. Elizabeth is humming with the activities of some 2,999 industries and businesses, it serves as the county seat for Union County, is the home of the Elizabeth Campus of Union County College, contains many auxiliary services for the seaport and airport, and has growing Hispanic, Portuguese, Asian, Caribbean, and Orthodox Jewish communities. Numerous urban renewal projects are replacing old housing and factories.

Despite all the changes and its position as fourth largest city in New Jersey, Elizabeth still has a small-town flavor where one meets one's neighbors on the street or on walks to the railroad stations. Westminster, Elmora, and Elmora Hills continue to be suburban with well-kept houses, while the small houses built for factory workers have been restored as town houses. Elizabeth has safe tree-shaded streets, pretty well-kept yards, attractive parks, and houses of worship for many religions. There are still people in the city who can trace their ancestry to the early settlers. Their children meet with those of the immigrants on the various playing fields and many teams in the city.

1. NEW JERSEY'S FIRST CAPITAL
1664–1775

The English settlers on Long Island and in Connecticut and Massachusetts looked longingly at the lush meadows, bubbling streams, ample wildlife and fish, primeval forests, sheltered coves, and unoccupied land near New Amsterdam. Twice delegates visited Governor Peter Stuyvesant in New Amsterdam requesting permission to settle on the land. He didn't say yes and he didn't say no.

Colonel Richard Nicolls, sailing for the British, seized New Amsterdam from the Dutch in October 1664. The would-be settlers requested his permission to settle on the land. He was happy to see them because King Charles II had urged him to settle the property after New Amsterdam was captured. The settlers, called Associates, were experienced colonists. Many of them had established homes and farms in Massachusetts, Connecticut, or the eastern end of Long Island.

To maintain good relations with the Lenape Indians, the settlers purchased land from Matano and his Sachems (leading officials of the tribe) on Staten Island. They paid for the Elizabethtown purchase with twenty fathoms of trading cloth, two coats, two guns, two kettles, ten bars of lead, and twenty handfuls of powder. A year after settling on the land, the settlers agreed to pay the Native Americans 400 fathoms of white wampum. (A fathom measures 6 feet. Wampum was a string of small beads made of shells and used by North American Indians as money and as ornaments. Black wampum was considered more valuable than white wampum.) The total paid to the Indians was about £154 for 500,000 acres of land. It was a generous bargain. The purchase covered all of present day Essex and Union Counties and portions of Passaic, Morris, Somerset, and Middlesex Counties.

Dr. Herbert Kraft of Seton Hall University found that the Lenapes and other Indian tribes lacked the concept of land ownership. The Lenapes, who were farmers, grew their crops and moved on to other land when they felt it was necessary. The new settlers maintained friendly relations with the Lenapes. The Lenapes unfortunately were susceptible to white man's diseases and many caught them and died. Efforts by the white settlers to enslave them later failed. They simply disappeared into the woods. Dr. Kraft declared that the phrase Lenni Lenape is unnecessary. Both words mean the same thing. Historians estimate that

Built c. 1724 by Captain Hunloke apparently for protection of the hamlet, this building was called "The Old Fort" and stood beside the Elizabeth River on Thompson's Lane. It was also the home of Cortland Van Ansdol and William Shute. It was demolished in 1932.

there were from 2,000 to 5,000 Indians in New Jersey at the time the white man began settling it. The land deeds were to John Bayley, Daniel Denton, Luke Watson, John Baker—who acted as the interpreter—and later John Ogden Sr., the oldest man to settle in the new colony.

Governor Nicolls, encouraged by the urgings of the settlers, granted them their rights as Englishmen. These were called the "Concessions and Agreements." They included religious freedom, the right to govern themselves in their own towns, free choices of officers both civilian and military, entitlement to town lots, the right to hold office and to vote. They were required to enforce the laws of the King and themselves. While religious freedom was guaranteed, the people were expected to be Protestant. Land was reserved in the hamlet for the clergyman.

The men drew for the town lots. These lots were 260 feet by 600 to 990 feet in size for house lots. The lots started at the Arthur Kill and moved up the Elizabethtown River to the head of tide at the Stone Bridge on today's Broad Street. The distance was about 2.5 miles along the winding river. The straighter road known as the King's Highway, Old York Road, Water Street, and finally Elizabeth Avenue was only about 2 miles distance to the Stone Bridge. The early settlers also drew for salt meadow land near the Arthur Kill and timber land inland on higher elevations. Youths as young as 14 years were allowed to participate in the drawings. Henry Lyon and his five sons, for instance, each drew for land. Lyon family members owned property extending from Lyon's Farms (South Ward of Newark and Hillside) to Rahway and westward toward First Mountain or the

Watchung Mountains. Lyon's Farms was named for the large number of people by the surname Lyon who lived in the area in the early eighteenth century.

According to legend, the head-of-tide site was selected as the center for the new community because pirates frequently raided coastal towns. Captain William Kidd, one of them, is said to have buried some of his treasure somewhere along the Arthur Kill before his capture in 1691.

One of the provisions of the "Concessions and Agreements" granted the settlers additional land if they owned slaves. No records exist regarding the ownership of slaves in the early settlement or when slave ownership began, although there reportedly was a slave market near the Stone Bridge. The New Jersey Archives contain copies of newspaper advertisements from the eighteenth century with many mentions of slaves and bond servants who ran away from their masters. Cornelius Hatfield, who was a leader in the Presbyterian Church, was a slave trader before the Revolutionary War. Several owners freed slaves in their wills during the eighteenth century, including those of Abraham Clark, a signer of the Declaration of Independence. Early records of the area were lost in fires or discarded by former householders who kept them in their homes. A few survive at the Princeton University library.

Bond servants were granted free passage on ships either by the sea captain, the ship's owner, or a local resident. When they arrived in Elizabethtown they were usually assigned to the person who had paid the fare and given up to seven years' labor to work off the fee. At the conclusion of their bondage, they were provided with a plot of land and their freedom.

Four families arrived in December 1664 and apparently built sod houses to live in until spring, when additional families came and began to build wood frame houses. The seal of the City of Elizabeth shows the first four dwellings. Nobody knows who the first residents were. Many of the early houses started as one-story, one-room shelters with an attic or loft. They grew as the family and its finances increased. Before the Revolutionary War, visitors were praising Elizabethtown for being the most attractive hamlet. Each two-story dwelling had its own kitchen garden and a few fruit trees. Many had wells for water and necessary houses (outhouses) built in the rear of the properties. The houses were either wood timber from trees cut in the nearby forests or brick made from clay along the river. Fences surrounded the houses and the pastures. The settlement was the first English-speaking community in New Jersey.

In July 1665, the settlers learned that Captain Sir Philip Carteret was enroute to the hamlet representing Sir George Carteret and John Lord Berkeley, the new proprietors of the area. King Charles II gave the land to his brother James, the Duke of York and future King James II of England. James was in debt to Berkeley and Carteret. He donated the future New Jersey to them in payment of these debts. (The proprietors divided the land: Sir George became the proprietor of East Jersey and Lord Berkeley the proprietor of West Jersey.)

Carteret sailed his ship the *Philip* into the Arthur Kill, anchored it off the Point, and waded ashore on August 1. Like King Charles II, the new proprietors were eager for the land to be settled. The arrival of the 26-year-old youthful captain was pleasant. He immediately became an Associate and shouldered a hoe to indicate that he would work with the Associates. He was accompanied by 30 people including 18 servants and some women. Robert Vauquellin was appointed surveyor general of the new colony by the proprietors. James Bollen was Philip's secretary and served in Carteret's place when he was absent.

Carteret named the hamlet Elizabethtown for his cousin, Lady Elizabeth Carteret, wife of another cousin, Sir George Carteret. He named the area New Jersey for his home Isle of Jersey in the English Channel. Governor Carteret also purchased the land of John Bayley, becoming a true Associate. He told the other Associates that one-seventh of the land in the colony was to be reserved for the Proprietors. The Associates objected. Governor Carteret reserved land outside the hamlet for the Proprietors anyway.

Carteret anticipated collecting quitrents in five years to provide payment to the proprietors. He failed to realize that transactions in the colonies were paid for with bartered goods or services, not with cash. There were few hard coins in the colonies. This condition lasted until the beginning of the nineteenth century. English or Spanish coins were used when they could be acquired.

Most of the people from the Isle of Jersey were French and Roman Catholic, while most of the Associates were English and Congregationalists (United Church of Christ or Independents). While Roman Catholic priests occasionally visited the hamlet in the eighteenth century, Roman Catholics who desired to attend Mass would either travel to New York City, Staten Island, or after 1826, to Newark. Most, if they wanted to attend church, went to the Congregational Church until the Episcopal Church was founded in 1705. The two religious groups appear to have lived peacefully with each other.

In 1666, representatives of the New Haven Colony approached Governor Carteret and asked for permission to settle on the bay, eventually known as Newark Bay, and the river, named the Passaic River. Carteret granted the permission. Three ships commanded by Captain Robert Treat arrived with colonists, household goods, and farm animals to settle Newark, named for the hometown of the colonists' minister, Reverend Abraham Pierson Sr. Unlike Elizabethtown, which was Puritanical but permitted all freemen the right to vote, Newark was a theocracy and required church membership to hold office or to vote. Newark's theocracy, an attempt to create heaven on earth, lasted briefly.

Reverend Pierson delayed his arrival until 1667, when he came with settlers of Connecticut Farms (Union). Elizabethtown meanwhile built a meeting house on the site of the present First Presbyterian Church on Broad Street and used it as a fort or general meeting house six days a week and a sanctuary on Sundays. No records of a clergyman conducting Sunday service exists until Reverend Jeremiah Peck's arrival in 1668, after three years in Newark, to become pastor in Elizabethtown. Both communities claim to have started the first church. Oddly the people from Connecticut Farms attended church service in Elizabethtown because the church was closer than Newark until they built their own church in the 1730s.

This post-Revolutionary building for the First Presbyterian Church of Elizabeth replaced an earlier one that burned in an English raid during the Revolutionary War.

Governor Carteret initially feared relations with the Lenapes, but they were peaceful. In 1759, the first Indian reservation in the American colonies was established at Indian Mills (Brotherton). The Native Americans sold their land in 1801 and moved to Lake Oneida, New York. Remnants of the Lenapes moved to Oklahoma. The Indians who reside in New Jersey today are from other tribes.

The legislature met at Governor Carteret's white house on May 28, 1668, making Elizabethtown the first capital of New Jersey. There were two burgesses from each of the new English colonies including Woodbridge, Piscataway, Newark, Middletown, Shrewsbury, and Bergen. Elizabethtown's representatives were John Ogden Sr. and John Bracket, for whom Bracket's Brook was named. Among the laws adopted was one placing drunkards and other wrongdoers in the stocks in front of the courthouse for all to see. Other laws outlined the treatment of children and bond servants. The assembly also approved commissioners to oversee land distribution, plan roads, determine landings, provide for operation of ferries, establish a militia, and construct bridges, jails, and animal pounds.

The upper house was appointed by Governor Carteret and included Captain John Berry, William Pardon, Robert Vauquellin, and James Bollen. All of these men had come on the *Philip* with Carteret. Later Robert Bond and Richard Townley were added. Historians criticize Carteret for failure to include more of the settlers in his council. It usually included only Frenchmen, who came with him.

The Puritan tradition was very strong in Elizabethtown. Unnecessary travel was prohibited and only necessary labor such as feeding the livestock was performed on Sundays. Since few people owned horses or carriages, they walked to church. Two two-hour long services were held each Sunday, one in the morning and the other in the afternoon. Housewives were forbidden to cook on the Lord's Day. Consequently cooking and food preparation was done on Saturdays. The women would pack picnic lunches for their families to eat after the morning service. The intermission between services gave the people an opportunity to gossip with relatives and friends before they returned home to another week of chores. Since there was no heat in the meeting house, the pastor would call a recess, during which time the congregation could visit a local tavern to get warm. Oddly enough, alcoholic beverages were acceptable. Wine and beer were among them. Footwarmers were permitted in the church.

One Sunday a Miller family from the west fields of Elizabethtown (Westfield) was honored at a service because they had moved to the west fields and it was assumed that they would no longer attend church services. The following Sunday, the family was seated in its usual pew, having walked the 10 miles to be there.

The few existing roads were muddy or rocky. The roads originally were animal paths, then Indian trails, routes followed by the Dutch fur traders and finally used by the Elizabethans to reach other hamlets. Oxen were used to help the farmers on their farms, but not for long-distance travel. Since most of the early settlements were along the coast, shallow-draft boats were the preferred vehicle for transportation. Most people traveled by boat if they wanted to go long distances.

John Ogden Sr., at 56 years, was the oldest man in the settlement and a master of all trades. Earlier he was among the founders of Stamford, Connecticut in 1641, and built a brick church in New Haven with his brother Richard. He moved to Hempstead, Long Island three years later and then to Northampton. He was requested to participate in the settlement on the Arthur Kill. His five grown sons came with him and participated in the land drawings. In Elizabethtown, he built first a lumber mill and later a grist mill close to the Old Stone Bridge over the Elizabethtown River connecting today's Broad and South Broad Streets. He made bricks and is said to have built several brick houses. He opened a tannery and helped to make Elizabethtown an important leather producing area. He also served as justice of peace.

Ogden organized a whaling company licensed by Governor Carteret for three years for whaling rights from Sandy Hook to Barnegat Bay. In return the company was to pay the governor one-twentieth of all the oil in casks. Whaling was done from small boats. When someone on land, perhaps mounted on a tall pole erected for the purpose, spotted a whale, the harpooner would throw the harpoon at the whale. A lance was used to administer the death blow. The dead whale was towed to shore, where the blubber was cut off and boiled down for valuable oil. The keratin was used for corset stays, whips, and later umbrella ribs The spermaceti was used for candles. Whales were common and were often seen offshore.

The location of the boundary between Elizabethtown and Newark was determined by representatives of both hamlets in 1668. Elizabethtown was represented by John Ogden Sr., Luke Watson, Robert Bond, and Jeffrey Jones.

The men met at Divident Hill, a round hill above a swamp opposite the Road to Lyons Farms (Lyons Avenue, Newark) from Camptown (Irvington). They started the boundary line at the The Upper Road to Newark (or Elizabeth depending on the direction traveled). The border extended through the swamp to Bound Creek at the head of the cove in the future Weequahic Park Lake. Bound Creek was used by flat-bottom boats in the seventeenth and eighteenth centuries. There were docks on both sides of the creek. One was for Newark and the other for Elizabethtown. Bound Creek emptied into Newark Bay. Now it goes through the Elizabeth Channel at the seaport into Newark Bay.

Many of the people were well-known craftsmen. They included Richard Painter and Robert Morss, tailors; Caleb Carwithy, a mariner; William Cramer, a carpenter; Matthias Hatfield, boatman and weaver; John and James Hinds, coopers, persons who make or repair barrels and casks; and Isaac Whitehead, a cordwainer, maker of shoes.

Reverend Jeremiah Peck followed a strict Puritanical code. There is no record of how the congregation felt about him during the ten years he served it, but he was forced to leave the ministry at his next church in Greenwich, Connecticut because he wanted all church members to testify to true conversion to Christianity.

The era of good-will between the Associates and the Proprietors was brief. The Proprietors wanted a profit from their investment. The young governor was directed to collect the quitrents including the peppercorn. The colonists refused to

Divident Hill in Weequahic Park is the traditional border between Elizabethtown and Newark. Representatives of both hamlets met on this knoll above the marshland in 1668 to determine the boundary. This structure was erected in 1916.

15

pay them, saying that they received the land from the Lenapes and paid the Lenapes for it. The quitrents went unpaid until the Revolutionary War wiped out the debt.

The colonists also protested when Governor Carteret made Richard Michell, a bond servant, an Associate after he completed his term of service. The next morning eight of the Associates ripped down Michell's fence. A group of men returned the next day and pulled boards off Michell's house and let his hogs loose. Eight Associates were arrested, tried, and found guilty. William Meeker, accused of being the ring leader, was fined £5 and the others £3. Some time later, Carteret seized Meeker's property. His relatives and friends purchased another plot for him. His descendants became leaders in the area. One of them, Dr. William Rankin Ward Sr. of Newark, was president of both the Sons of the American Revolution and the New Jersey Historical Society.

The quiet of the hamlet was disturbed in 1672 when James Carteret, son of Sir George and Lady Elizabeth Carteret, arrived in Elizabethtown. The townspeople, angry with Governor Carteret, elected James the president of New Jersey. The two factions disagreed until Governor Carteret sailed for England. One of his supporters returned from England with papers stating that Philip was the legitimate governor and James must leave. John Berry, the deputy governor of New Jersey, served until Governor Philip Carteret returned. James Carteret left. Why his parents failed to support him or sent him in the first place is unknown. He was assigned to the Carolinas by his father. He boarded the *Samual Davis*, a sloop that was captured by the Dutch off Virginia. James and his wife were placed ashore to find their way to the Carolinas. Historians are uncertain as to his fate. One has him returning alone to New York and becoming a penniless alcoholic, while the other has him returning to England where he fathered a large family.

The Dutch recaptured New York City. Deputy Governor Berry surrendered New Jersey to the Dutch, who forced the Elizabethans to take oaths of allegiance to Holland and join the Dutch Reformed Church. They also were directed to send delegates to New Orange, as New York was called.

The people in Elizabethtown complied. They did not object to joining the church since both the Dutch Reformed and the Congregational churches followed the reformed tradition. They apparently felt they were far enough away from Holland to be free of their government. Before Dutch rule could become effective, the British recaptured New York and Governor Philip Carteret returned on November 6, 1674, resuming his position. The governor's council restored all land owned by the planters before the Dutch seized it.

Governor Carteret's problems were hardly over. His kinsman Sir Edmund Andros, governor of New York, claimed he had an order that made him governor of all territory between the Connecticut and Delaware Rivers. He wanted Carteret to leave his post. Carteret refused. One cold winter night in 1680, Andros's men paddled up the Elizabethtown River to Carteret's white house, forced entry, and seized Carteret in his nightshirt. Putting him in a canoe, they returned to New York where he was thrown in prison. He was charged with illegally exercising the office of governor of New Jersey and tried three times.

Each time, the jury found him innocent. Governor Andros declared himself governor of New Jersey anyway and escorted Carteret back to Elizabethtown, warning him not to govern.

The former governor apparently had had enough. Instead of fighting for his office, he began building a new brick home and courted and won a rich widow, Elizabeth Smith Lawrence of Long Island, mother of seven children, as his bride. Before the wedding, he signed probably the first prenuptial agreement in New Jersey promising that her estate would go to her sons. They married in April 1681. Governor Andros left for England and Philip resumed his governorship. He advised all persons who had suffered losses during the Andros term to file suits. The marriage and his term as governor were brief. Philip died a year later suffering from injuries received during his captivity. He was only 43. Philip granted his servant Black Jack his freedom in his will.

Reverend Seth Fletcher was selected as the second pastor of the Elizabethtown church after the pulpit was vacant for five years. He became embroiled in a theological discussion with a Quaker schoolmaster. He died in 1682, leaving a large library of books, which was rare for that time.

Thomas Rudyard became deputy governor of East New Jersey in November 1682, after Lady Elizabeth Carteret, widow of Sir George Carteret, sold her interest to 12 Quakers in London including William Penn, Thomas Rudyard, and Samuel Groome. This Lady Elizabeth never visited her namesake. Philip Carteret's widow, also a Lady Elizabeth Carteret, never visited the Isle of Jersey. The new proprietors selected Robert Barclay, a Scottish Quaker, as governor of East Jersey. Barclay never came to New Jersey. Rudyard governed in his place. Eventually the number of Quaker proprietors was increased to 24.

Reverend Dr. Edwin F. Hatfield in his book, *The History of Elizabeth, New Jersey*, notes that the Carterets represented the Stuart kings while Rudyard represented the Quakers, who were settling in the future Rahway and the western part of New Jersey along the Delaware River. The Quakers were plain people compared to the Stuarts. Puritanical Elizabethans found them more like themselves. Deputy Governor Rudyard also appointed members of the community to his council.

East Jersey was divided into four counties at the first council meeting. They became Essex, Monmouth, Middlesex, and Bergen Counties. Rudyard was replaced in July 1683, by Gawen Lawrie, a proprietor and associate of William Penn in West Jersey. The reason for the replacement is unclear. Lawrie was a merchant in London. He was accompanied to New Jersey by several associates each with servants, all Scottish, who were escaping the 1684 "killing time" in Scotland. He wrote home to London that all the area lacked was more people. He gave glowing reports on the streams, fields, acres of trees, peaches, strawberries, wildlife, and good soil. Most of the land around Elizabethtown was held by old families who desired to keep their land, and land titles once more were questioned. Purchase of land near the Blue Hills (Watchung Mountains behind present-day Scotch Plains) where earlier Scottish settlers were located further complicated land titles there.

Elizabethtown continued to be the capital until April 6, 1686, when a meeting was called at Amboy (later Perth Amboy) and it became the capital of East Jersey until the new nation, and later the state, were formed. The name Perth Amboy came into use after the Revolutionary War.

Lawrie was replaced by Lord Neill Campbell, a Presbyterian, from 1686 to 1687, when he was able to return home to Scotland. Captain Andrew Hamilton followed him in 1689. Sir Edmund Andros became the captain general of New England and once again ruler of New York and New Jersey. His tenure was brief. Hamilton became governor a second time and was followed by Governor Jermiah Basse in 1699, who served only two years, when Hamilton returned again.

Many Scottish laborers came to the area encouraged by Robert Barclay. Barclay granted permission to George Scot to send some Lowland Scots, who moved into Scot's Plains (Scotch Plains). Under an agreement 50 acres were given to each family and 25 more acres for each family member or indentured servant. Migration increased from Scotland during the reign of King James II from 1685 to 1688. William, Prince of Orange, and his wife Lady Mary, daughter of James II, became co-rulers of Great Britain in 1689. Land title disputes and court cases followed. In 1693, the boundaries of Elizabethtown were listed as extending across present day Union County and included portions of Somerset, Hunterdon, Morris, Warren, and Sussex Counties from Newark Bay for 44 miles inland and from the Raritan to the Passaic Rivers.

Queen Mary died in 1694, and her husband King William III in 1702. Her sister Queen Anne was the last of the Stuart monarchs. One of her first acts was to take control of New Jersey, ending the proprietors' rule and uniting the colony as one. She appointed her cousin Edward Hyde, Lord Cornbury, as governor both of New York and New Jersey. Lord Cornbury shocked the people by dressing in women's clothes. Queen Anne died in 1714. She was followed by her son King George I (1714–1747), and her grandson George II (1727–1760). George II granted a new charter for Elizabethtown Borough in 1738. Joseph Bonnel of Connecticut Farms became the first mayor. He represented Elizabethtown in the General Assembly from 1716 to 1743 and served as speaker in 1738. He also was named a judge of the Supreme Court.

The joint governorship continued until 1738, when Lewis Morris, a native of the colonies, was appointed governor of New Jersey. The organization of the proprietors had effectively ended although the East Jersey Proprietors continued until 1999, while the West Jersey Proprietors continues to exist. They own any land that is unclaimed. East Jersey developed as the center of population, transportation, industry, and commerce. West Jersey was agrarian until urban sprawl caught up with it toward the end of the twentieth century.

Reverend John Harriman, who appears to be something of a wheeler and dealer, became the Congregational Church's third pastor after a pulpit vacancy of five years. The colonies appeared to lack sufficient clergymen. One of Harriman's talents was the ability to work as a surveyor, which he did with Robert Vauquellin

The home of Nathaniel Bonnel at 1045 East Jersey Street is believed to be the oldest dwelling still standing in Elizabeth. Built before 1682, it later was the home of Colonel Francis Barber.

on the boundary line between the colonies of New York and Connecticut. Vauquellin may have been responsible for his coming to Elizabethtown.

Harriman kept careful records of the church's donations for his support. Most of the payments were in services such as labor on his farm, in his flour and cider mills or garden, building his house or barn, in shoemaking, weaving, or producing food. He also asked for and received a grant of 100 acres in addition to that already set aside for the clergyman. He provided glass to his neighbors, served as a deputy to the legislature, conducted a boarding school at his home, and dealt in real estate and the slave trade. Before he died in 1705, he was joined by the Reverend Samuel Melyen, who became the pastor after Reverend Harriman's death. Melyen was pastor briefly, then he quit. He died in 1709. The reason for his quitting is unknown.

In the meantime, Richard Townley arrived in the colonies in 1683 with Francis Howard, Lord Effingham, governor of Virginia. He left Virginia for Elizabethtown where he met Lady Elizabeth Carteret, marrying her in 1684. No prenuptial agreements were signed before this wedding. There are many New Jersey residents who are direct descendants of this union. Many of them have the name Richard Townley. Townley was an Anglican and a Jacobite, a supporter of James II.

Townley immediately became a leader in the community. He offered his home for services by Reverend John Brooke, an Episcopal priest. The house was the brick house built by Sir Philip Carteret for his bride. When the congregation outgrew the house, Townley provided his barn. When the barn became too small to handle the worshippers, Reverend Melyen offered the use of the Congregational church for Anglican services until they could build a church. They accepted. The only restriction placed on the Anglicans was that Reverend Brooke not read from the Book of Common Prayer at the services. Reverend Brooke solved that problem by memorizing the book. Colonel Townley donated land for St. John's Episcopal Church in 1711. Most of the Episcopal churches in the area today are offshoots of St. John's. Reverend Edward Vaughan followed Reverend Brooke in 1707. He married Townley's step-daughter Mary Lawrence Emmot, a widow.

Reverend Jonathan Dickinson was called as pastor of the Congregational Church in 1708, and the two clergymen cooperated with each other. Reverend Dickinson was interested in the Presbyterian movement and in time led his church into the Synod of Philadelphia in 1717. Reverend Dickinson served as clerk for the Presbytery of Philadelphia until he became active in the formation of the East New Jersey Presbytery in 1737, the same year that King George II chartered the Borough of Elizabethtown and James Bonnell of Connecticut Farms, speaker of the assembly, became the first mayor. The new borough extended to the Passaic River below Long Hill, formerly Millington. The Elizabeth church became known as the "mother of churches" as new churches were formed in Rahway, Westfield, and Springfield.

Reverend Dickinson directed the erection of a new church to replace the original one. He gained respect for his writings on religious subjects. He welcomed George Whitefield, leader of the Great Awakening. Whitefield's appearance created considerable controversy. He caused a division between the New Light and Old Light Presbyterians. The Old Light Presbyterians wanted new ministers to be trained in Yale or Harvard in New England.

The New Light Presbyterians including Reverend Aaron Burr Sr., Reverend Theodore J. Frelinghuysen, and Reverend Jonathan Dickinson wanted the new clergymen to be trained in New Jersey, which lacked a school. Reverend Aaron Burr Sr. and Reverend Jonathan Dickinson applied to Governor John Hamilton in 1746, after the death of Governor Lewis Morris, and received a charter for the College of New Jersey at Elizabethtown. Reverend Dickinson began to write in favor of evangelism. The Quakers and Anglicans opposed evangelists.

Unfortunately Reverend Dickinson died in his parsonage on Jelf's Hill a few months after the college opened and the college was moved to the parsonage of Reverend Aaron Burr Sr. at the Presbyterian Church in Newark.

Reverend Elihu Spencer, a kinsman of John Brainerd, an Indian missionary, was installed as pastor of the Presbyterian church in 1749. He served only seven years. During his service Elizabethtown once more became the Province's capital when Governor Jonathan Belcher moved from Burlington to Elizabethtown in 1751. Belcher, a native of the American colonies, believed that Elizabethtown would be better for his health than Burlington. His wife and step-daughter Elizabeth came to town and purchased the former Ogden house, now known as the Belcher-Ogden House at East Jersey Street, restored in the 1960s by the Elizabethtown Historical Foundation.

St. John's Episcopal Church was organized in 1705 and erected this building in 1774. It was used by both sides during the Revolutionary War for quartering troops, storing supplies, and stabling horses, and was badly damaged. It was razed in 1859 and replaced by a Gothic structure.

Elizabeth supervised the enlargement of the house and stocked it with good wines and beer, 60 cords of wood for the five fireplaces, 12 barrels of cider, apples, pears, vegetables, and flour, and made provisions for the family's cows. Three sloops carried the Belcher family furniture up the Elizabeth River to a landing in back of the house.

Governor Belcher enjoyed entertaining. An alcove in the east bedroom was designed as a study with a large desk and shelves for books. Reverend Jonathan Edwards, grandfather of Aaron Burr Jr., is said to have used the study frequently when visiting Governor Belcher. Reverend Edwards was known as "The hell fire and brimstone preacher." He started the Great Awakening in his church in Northampton, Massachusetts, in 1734. His most famous sermon was "Sinners in the Hands of an Angry God," at Enfield, Connecticut in 1741. On June 22, 1750, he was dismissed from the pastorate of the Northampton church. He became a missionary to the Native Americans at Stockbridge, Massachusetts. In 1753, he published an essay "On the Freedom of The Will." Three years later, after the death of his son-in-law Reverend Aaron Burr Sr., he became the president of the College of New Jersey and moved it to Princeton. His presidency was brief because he succumbed to small pox. The college became Princeton University in 1890. The present College of New Jersey, the former Trenton State College, has nothing to do with the original.

Other guests were friends Governor Belcher made while serving as governor of Massachusetts. He conducted meetings of the council in his dwelling. When he was well, they were in a room on the first floor. When he was ailing, he held them in his bedchamber. He died in 1757.

Reverend Spencer was followed by Reverend Abraham Keteltas, who began preaching in 1756 at the Presbyterian church. He was ordained and installed as pastor of the church September 14, 1757, and served three and a half years. The reason for his leaving is not disclosed. He soon withdrew from the Presbytery. His ability to speak both French and Dutch made him popular among people speaking those languages and he frequently preached from pulpits in Dutch or French Huguenot churches.

Mayor Bonnel was followed by Samuel Woodruff, who served as mayor from 1748 to 1762 and built Boxwood Hall; John DeHart, a lawyer, from 1762 to 1772; and Stephen Crane, an ancestor of the author of *The Red Badge of Courage*, from 1772 to 1774.

Several men served as governors briefly after Governor Belcher's death. Among them were John Reading, Francis Bernard, Nathaniel Jones, Thomas Boone, and Josiah Hardy.

In the meantime there were frequent wars between England and the French that spread to the American colonies and the Native Americans. As a result British troops were billeted from time to time in the residents' homes under the Quartering Act. The householder was expected to provide food, shelter, and other necessities for the soldier. The people objected. Finally five barracks were built in 1756 in Trenton—the only one still standing, New Brunswick, Elizabethtown, Perth Amboy, and Burlington. In peace time, the barracks provided a source of income for the merchants and a social outlet such as dances for the young ladies of the town. Many of the officers stationed at the barracks were related to residents of Elizabethtown.

William Bradford, who is considered to be the first colonial printer by some historians, operated a shop in Elizabethtown briefly before he moved it to Amboy. He also had a papermill on the Elizabeth River that is believed to have been the first in the colonies. He supplied paper for the *New York Gazette*, circulated in Elizabethtown. The newspaper began in 1725 and continued through the Revolutionary War. His son Andrew printed another newspaper, *The American Weekly Mercury*. New Jersey lacked a newspaper of its own until Isaac Collins began the *New Jersey Gazette* in Burlington on December 5, 1777. He moved it to Trenton where it continued to be published as the *State Gazette* until 1942.

While most of the people continued to farm, keep cattle and chickens, grow fruit trees and vegetable gardens, and serve in the military, many also became craftsmen or followed other occupations. Their houses in the center of the hamlet served as both their homes and shops. Occupations varied: Vincent Runyon and William Cramer were carpenters; Robert Blackwell was a merchant; John Brackett Sr. was a surveyor; Evan Salisbury was both a brickmaker and a carpenter; Peter Couvenhoven was a brewer and keeper of an ordinary (tavern);

This painting in the First Presbyterian Church museum shows the home of former mayor John DeHart at 101 Rahway Avenue. The house was built c. 1745.

while Peter Wolversen, a Dutchman, operated a brewery and tavern; Pierre Jardine, a Frenchman, kept an inn; and Jonas Wood operated a tavern.

Additional craftsmen continued to work in Elizabethtown including David Ross, a bell maker; Aaron Miller, maker of clocks; Jonathan Dayton, a tailor; Abraham Hetfield and John Ross, cordwainers; David Marsh, a millwright; Jonathan Morrell, nailmaker; Ebenezer Spining, cooper; Matthias and Benjamin Halsted, silversmiths; Geishom Higgins, Joseph Little, and Baker Hendricks, blacksmiths; Aaron Lane, silversmith; Jonathan Higgins, coachmaker; and Elias Boudinot III, silversmith.

William Franklin, the natural son of Benjamin Franklin, was appointed New Jersey's last royal governor in May 1763. He held the title until the colonists declared their independence on July 4, 1776, and he failed to cooperate with them. He was arrested and sent to a prison at New Windsor, Connecticut. Released in October 1778, he was allowed to go to New York City, where he stayed until he moved to England in 1782. Efforts by his father to change his mind from supporting the royalty failed.

The area's grievances against the British crown were many. The question of land titles continued to plague the people, because they believed they had valid titles. Some had managed to get titles from both the Associates and Proprietors. Efforts to reach a compromise for the others appeared futile. The British harassed them for quitrents, which the people refused to pay.

The merchants disliked the restrictions on trade. Ships sailing from Elizabethtown were required to stop at England first before going to European ports. There were restrictions too on trade with the Caribbean islands. The British also issued a proclamation banning additional settlements west of the

Allegheny Mountains. The crown wanted to approve all land grants within Native-American territory.

All colonial appointees such as judges had to be approved by the crown. Laws known as the hat, wool, and iron acts were adopted to protect British commerce from competition in the colonies.

Most of all there were the taxes. The many wars that the English were fighting were costly, and various methods were used to gain more income. One of the first of these was the Molasses Act, which imposed duties upon sugar, molasses, and rum imported by the colonies from the West Indies in 1733. The Sugar Act of 1764 placed a tax on sugar. Honey or molasses could be used to replace sugar and was. The Sugar Act also imposed duties on colonial imports such as textiles, coffee, indigo, and wines.

In 1750, England prohibited further building of slitting or rolling mills in the colonies. Only pig and bar iron were allowed. These were to be sent to England duty free. Most mine owners ignored the laws on iron. Copper mined in Newark was supposed to be taken to England to be refined before it could be used. Instead, foundries were hidden in the woods and copper was refined there, escaping the law.

Benjamin Franklin twice attempted to gain unification of the colonies under one head appointed by the crown. It was denied. James Otis, a Boston lawyer,

The West Room of the Belcher-Ogden Mansion features Delft tiles around the fireplace. The room was used by Governor Belcher for council meetings.

attempted to prohibit customs officials from using general search warrants and urged that the American colonists have the same legal rights as those provided to the British. He also protested taxation without representation, which became one of the watchwords of the Revolution.

The Currency Act of 1764 prohibited the colonies from issuing paper money and limited the amount of paper money in circulation in the counties. It was ignored because there was little paper money anyway. Most of the people bartered their services or crops for the articles they wanted or used British or Spanish coins.

The Massachusetts legislature organized a Committee of Correspondence to keep in touch with the other 12 colonies and to express grievances against such laws as the Sugar Act. The idea grew and hamlets such as Elizabethtown established their own Committees of Correspondence to keep in touch with other communities in New Jersey. Boston merchants too introduced the policy of non-importation of British goods, which eventually spread to Elizabethtown.

The Stamp Act, requiring a stamp on all legal papers, was adopted March 22, 1765. The reaction against the act was both hostile and swift. It was immediately opposed by lawyers, merchants, publishers, shipowners, real estate owners, speculators, tavern owners, and insurance companies. The local Sons of Liberty in Elizabethtown erected a gallows in front of the courthouse and promised to hang anyone who purchased one of the stamps. Nobody did. The opposition to the various taxes and the increased cry by the legislatures for the colonies to govern themselves caused the formation of Sons of Liberty groups by 1765 in many of the hamlets. Originally started by the merchants and leaders of the hamlets, some became violent as they forced the resignation of stamp agents and the cancellation of orders for merchandise from England.

Robert Ogden of Elizabethtown, speaker of the Assembly, called a special meeting of the Assembly at Amboy to select delegates to attend a Continental Congress without Governor Franklin's approval. One of the main objections to the Stamp Act was that it was approved by Parliament without consulting the provinces. It encouraged the cry "No taxation without representation!" The colonists believed that taxes should be imposed by their own legislatures.

Meanwhile three delegates including Ogden, Hendrick Fisher, and Joseph Borden were sent from the New Jersey Legislature unofficially to a meeting of the Continental Congress in New York City to protest the Stamp Act and petition for its repeal. Their attendance was unofficial because Governor Franklin disapproved. The Stamp Act was repealed as a result of the storm of protests and the reduction of English imports by the American merchants.

Charles Townshend, chancellor of the Exchequer, had the British Parliament replace the stamp act with a series of nuisance taxes on wine, oil, fruit, glass, paper, lead, painters' colors, and tea. These were called the Townshend Acts. These new duties were just as odious as the Stamp Act. The Essex County Freeholders (Elizabethtown was a part of Essex County until 1857) adopted resolutions agreeing that merchants and traders would not import any of the listed items. The

Committee of Correspondence was directed to keep watch on cargoes of ships and merchandise in shops to prevent backsliding by the merchants.

Two regiments of English infantry sailed into Boston from Nova Scotia in an effort to quell Boston's passionate refusal to import British goods. Delegates to an unofficial conference at Faneuil Hall decided to arm. In a confrontation on March 5, 1770 between the soldiers and a mob in Boston, three persons were killed, two mortally wounded, and six injured. One of the persons killed was an African American, Crispus Attucks, a sailor. The shooting became known as the Boston Massacre. The British company that participated in the Boston Massacre later was transferred to the Barracks in Elizabethtown.

The Townshend Acts were repealed, but the Essex County merchants voted to continue their non-importation agreement. A Tea Act was adopted by Parliament permitting the British East India Company to sell directly to the American colonies. On December 16, 1773, a group of men in Boston dressed as Native Americans dumped tea from a ship into Boston Harbor. The event became known as the Boston Tea Party. The action was duplicated at the College of New Jersey at Princeton, where the students broke into the college's tea supply and burned it, and at Greenwich, New Jersey where residents, copying the people in Boston, dressed as Indians, broke into a storehouse containing tea and burned it on the village green.

Robert J. Fridlington in his book *Union County Yesterday* tells the story about nine-year-old Susan Boudinot, daughter of Elias and Hannah Stockton Boudinot, who was taken by her parents for a visit at the home of Royal Governor William Franklin at Westminster, the governor's home in Amboy. She must have heard the stories of the tea burnings in her home because she didn't want to drink the tea when it was served, but she didn't want to offend her host either. She raised the cup to her lips then walked across the room and tossed the contents out an open window. She had not tasted the despised tea.

Parliament retaliated to the actions in Boston by adopting the Boston Port Bill, the first of the Intolerable Acts, closing the port to all commercial shipping. Merchants such as Elias Dayton, who operated several trading ships along the coast, feared that Parliament would take the same action in Elizabethtown. The Committee of Correspondence at a meeting in New Brunswick decided to ask Governor Franklin to call a meeting of the General Assembly. He refused.

At another meeting of the committee in New Brunswick, the delegates rejected the Intolerable Acts as repugnant and urged the people of New Jersey to send money to help the people of Boston. They also adopted resolutions boycotting British goods. William Livingston, John DeHart, and Stephen Crane were among the five men named as deputies to the Continental Congress.

The first congress adopted non-importation and non-exportation agreements against Great Britain and urged the other colonies to do the same. The Committee of Correspondence in Essex County asked that Committees of Observation be formed in Elizabethtown, Newark, and Acquackanonk. The Committee of Observation in Elizabethtown urged residents to boycott the *Royal*

Gazette published by John Rivington in New York City. Rivington was thought to be a British spy. His newspaper favored the Tories throughout the coming war.

When Governor Franklin refused to call a meeting of the General Assembly, Robert Ogden called it. The General Assembly drew up a petition and sent it to King George III listing the grievances of the colonists. They continued to pledge their loyalty to the king. Robert Ogden, seeking both to keep the peace and have the colonies unified, told the assembly members that he thought the petition should be sent to each provincial legislature first for its approval. He was hung in effigy in Elizabethtown.

Robert Ogden, a lawyer, served in many capacities in Elizabethtown, such as clerk of the Court of Common Pleas for Essex County, recorder for the Borough of Elizabethtown, register for the Court of Chancery, member of the Governor's Council, Judge of the Essex County Court, surrogate of the Orphans Court of New Jersey, operator of the Ogden tanyard, ruling elder of the New York Synod of the Presbyterian Church, and as an active member of the Elizabethtown Presbyterian Church. His popularity disappeared for a time as war clouds gathered. The hamlet once more respected him, but he resigned from the Assembly and moved to Sussex County. The place he settled became known as Ogdensburg.

By the time of the Revolution, the Elizabethtown area included descendants of the settlers of New England, Scottish persons from Scotland, English, French, Dutch, a few Germans, and a few Scotch-Irish, persons born in North Ireland, but descendants of Scottish Highlanders, who never saw Scotland. Early Germans were accompanied by German Jews and a few are listed in the rolls of the Revolutionary War in New Jersey, but none is listed as coming from Elizabethtown. By the time of the Revolution there were several Jewish settlements in the colonies including Philadelphia, New York City, and Newport, Rhode Island. There also was an undetermined number of African Americans. Some of these were free, others were serving as apprentices to the various craftsmen. The rest were slaves. There were Presbyterians and Episcopalians in the hamlet. Quakers had settled in the Rahway and Plainfield areas of Elizabethtown. Baptists had settled at Scot's Plains, where a Baptist church was founded in 1747, and in Lyon's Farms, where the Lyon's Farms Baptist Church was organized in 1769. All of the early Baptist churches in Union and Essex Counties are said to have started in these churches.

War clouds were gathering. Efforts by moderates such as Robert Ogden were ignored. The only question was when it would begin.

2. A New Nation
1770–1800

Elizabethtown has been called the "Gateway to the Revolution" because people passed through it from the New York ferries to the highways to Philadelphia or the West. New Jersey is known as "The Crossroads of the Revolution" for much the same reason because travelers and armies went from Elizabethtown to Trenton and Philadelphia. It is called the "Cockpit of the Revolution" because there were so many battles or skirmishes during the eight-year war. More than 100 of these occurred in the Elizabethtown area alone. Another 196 engagements are recorded in New Jersey. Many of them are unknown or ignored because they lacked someone to tell about them. New Jersey, with its bountiful farms, good cattle, and fat hens, made it the bread basket for the Revolution for both the British and American troops.

Dennis P. Ryan, in his *New Jersey in the American Revolution, 1763–1783*, wrote:

> With the arrival of British troops and ships in New York Harbor [in July, 1776], New Jersey became the arena in which the battle for American independence was fought and won. Equally important, fighting continued in New Jersey for almost two years after the British surrender at Yorktown [October 19, 1781]. No state suffered more from military conflict, material devastation and civil war.

The war between 1776 and 1783 has been called both a Civil War and a Revolution. As a Civil War it was between political factions—the Royalists, Loyalists, or Tories who supported the crown, and the Patriots, Rebels, or Continentals who sought to govern themselves. As a Revolution, the government ruled by a king was overthrown and a new republican and democratic government was put in its place by force of arms.

The Patriots in Elizabethtown were wary of the people on Staten Island because they believed they were all Tories. When James Johnson of Staten Island sailed up the Elizabethtown River with a load of oysters to sell, his skiff and oysters were seized. Johnson sought help from Jonathan Hampton, chairman of the

Committee of Observation, who released the oysters for sale. In the evening Johnson's skiff was returned to him and he was permitted to leave.

In February 1775, two New York Quaker merchants, Robert and John Murray, attempted to smuggle two tons of cargo from their ship, the *Beulah*, into Elizabethtown. They sailed to Sandy Hook, where they had the cargo put in a sloop. The sloop was sailed to Elizabethtown where it was to be unloaded. Unfortunately for the Murrays, they were observed and reported. The cargo was confiscated. They donated £200 and pleaded for forgiveness. The pounds and their pleas were accepted.

While the battles of Lexington, Concord, and Bunker Hill were sparking the Revolutionary War in Massachusetts, the people in Elizabethtown were choosing sides. Reverend James Caldwell, who became known as the "fighting parson," was installed as pastor of the Presbyterian Church in 1762. He became chaplain of Colonel Elias Dayton's Third Battalion when Dayton was directed to guard the Mohawk Valley from a Native-American or British attack.

Pastor Caldwell was outspoken in his opposition to the crown along with other Presbyterian ministers in the Province of New Jersey. The others included Reverend John Witherspoon, president of the College of New Jersey and the only clergyman to sign the Declaration of Independence; Reverend Alexander Macwhorter, pastor the Presbyterian Church in Newark; Reverend Aaron Richards, pastor of the Presbyterian Church in Rahway; and Reverend Jedidiah Chapman, pastor of the First Mountain Society Church in the future Orange, who was called "The Rebel High Priest" by the British. The war became known as the Presbyterian War.

Reverend Thomas Bradbury Chandler followed Reverend Vaughn in the pulpit of St. John's Episcopal Church in December 1747. St. John's purchased the house overlooking the Elizabeth River as its parsonage and the vicar married Mary Emott, a daughter of Captain John Emott and Mary Boudinot Emott. He was a missionary to people living outside of the hamlet, covering some 3,000 miles a year according to Reverend Edwin F, Hatfield, D.D. (The St. John's Parsonage was restored by the Elizabethtown Historical Foundation and given to Union County. It is occupied by the Union County Division of Culture and Heritage Affairs.)

Reverend Chandler asked for and was granted a charter for the church on July 19, 1762. He refused to permit George Whitefield, the evangelist, to preach in the church. This denial caused a division in his congregation. Although he had not written pamphlets before, Reverend Chandler began to issue some supporting the crown. By 1775, the people of the hamlet were upset by his writing and sermons against the Americans. The church was guarded at night by church members to avoid vandalism. When war broke out, Reverend Chandler sailed to England, leaving his wife in the parsonage. He stayed in England until the war ended, then came back to Elizabethtown. According to church historians, half of the congregation supported the crown and the other half served with the Continental Army.

The people thought that Mrs. Chandler might be a spy because every British officer that passed through Elizabethtown stopped to visit her. The authorities never questioned her and she stayed in the parsonage through the war.

Mrs. Chandler was not alone in her assumed support of the British. Cavalier Jouet, a vestryman at St. John's and probably the richest man in Elizabethtown, was outspoken in his criticism of the coming war. Although he signed a paper pledging his allegiance to the new nation, he later removed his name to show his contempt. The Committee of Safety sent him to Basking Ridge when hostilities began and demanded that he post a bond to guarantee his good conduct. When General Washington began his retreat in 1776, Jouet began collecting information for the British about the Patriots. Because of this, he was forced to flee to New York City when the Continental Army reoccupied Elizabethtown. He later went to England and was ordained an Episcopal priest. He twice attempted to rejoin his family at war's end, but each time he was rejected. The land he inherited from his grandfather in Elizabethtown was confiscated.

Both sides had their spies. Elias Boudinot, who was in charge of prisoner exchange at Elizabethtown Point, and Colonel Elias Dayton were both thought to be spies. The Mersereau family of Staten Island was one of the busiest and most interesting. The family lived among the Tories and the British and Hessian armies. Members of the family would go fishing. When they arrived at Shooter's Island, just north of Staten Island, under the cover of darkness, one of them would place a message for the Continental Army under a designated rock. A Patriot from Elizabethtown who also was busy fishing would pick it up and deliver it to the intended recipient.

General Washington passed through Elizabethtown in June 1775 enroute to the hills outside of Boston to take command of the army. At Elizabethtown, he was advised to cross the Hudson River at Hoboken because the mayor of New York was arriving in the city from England on the same day, June 25. Nothing happened. The two men met separately with their admirers and the new commander-in-chief continued his uneventful trip to Cambridge, arriving on July 3. General Washington inspected the men and the camp. He was upset by what he saw. The men were badly in need of ammunition, clothes, and food. The three-month enlistments were expiring and many of the men were drifting away. A few reenlisted.

Washington wrote back to Elizabethtown and was sent gunpowder from the old mill by the river. The old mill was reactivated as a powder mill. Additional powder was collected in New Jersey and sent to him from Elizabethtown. He also began writing the first of many letters to the Continental Congress requesting money and supplies.

Several men such as Thomas Paine and William Livingston, the future New Jersey governor, were busy writing pamphlets and letters protesting the offenses of the British against the colonies. Paine's pamphlet *Common Sense* made him famous on both sides of the Atlantic. Livingston, a lawyer, purchased land for his estate, Liberty Hall, on the edge of Elizabethtown in 1772. He moved into the mansion in 1773. He wrote numerous letters to newspapers using pseudonyms, protesting the various taxes and protesting the failure of the crown to give the colonists representation on the various governing bodies including the Parliament.

Brigadier General Elias Dayton became the highest ranking officer in the Continental army in New Jersey when General William Maxwell resigned. A veteran of the French and Indian Wars who also served throughout the Revolution, he operated Elias Dayton and Son and served eight terms as mayor of Elizabeth.

The Provincial Assembly directed that each county form companies of militiamen. All men between 16 and 50 were to be included. The men in turn would elect their own officers and supply their own muskets, bayonets, swords, tomahawks, ramrods, pruning irons, cartridge boxes, 23 rounds, 12 flints, and a knapsack. The men were to keep their rifles at readiness at home with 1 pound of powder and 3 pounds of bullets at all times. Recruits were given a bonus of a felt hat, stockings, and shoes. Later in the war they were given small cash bonuses. The women of the hamlet were urged to spin and weave and were ordered not to kill young ewes.

The new militia, including 16 companies of foot and one of horse belonging to Elizabethtown, was reviewed on the parade ground in front of the courthouse, Presbyterian church, and Academy on October 4, 1775. They went through military exercises with alertness and regularity and made a very handsome appearance, an observer wrote.

William Alexander, Lord Stirling, William Livingston's brother-in-law, was appointed commander of the First New Jersey Regiment of Regulars. Earlier he had gone to Scotland in an attempt to gain the family title and had been refused. Despite that, he used the title and the family's coat of arms was painted on his coach. He also was a colonel of the Somerset County militia regiment. He sought to enforce a law that required all vessels entering New York Harbor to stop first at Amboy or Elizabethtown. Lord Stirling drilled the recruits on the parade ground.

Martha Washington and her party were escorted through Elizabethtown to Newark by a company of Light Horse and leading men of the community on November 19, 1775, on her way to join the general in Massachusetts. She spent every winter of the war with her husband. When spring came she returned to

31

Mount Vernon to oversee the operation of the plantation. She was a guest of the Livingstons at Liberty Hall on her first trip North. The Livingstons had a bedroom on the second floor built just for her. It became the room of John Kean, chairman of the board of directors of NUI, a gas company, when he was a youth.

In January 1776, Lord Stirling learned that the British cargo ship the *Blue Mountain Valley* was anchored at Prince's Bay on the southern shore of Staten Island. He selected a group of men to ride with him to Amboy to capture it. Shortly after they left Elizabethtown, it was learned that a company of British soldiers was taking the same route. Fearing that Alexander and his company would be captured, Colonel Elias Dayton acquired three boats and 100 men to attempt to head them off. Instead of sailing down the Arthur Kill, the men went around Staten Island and approached the *Blue Mountain Valley* from the sea just as the sun rose.

The sailors on board the ship apparently thought the three boats were fishermen returning to port after a night's fishing and the ship was captured before any of the sailors could act. Dayton met Lord Stirling and his men and the ship was sailed to Elizabethport. The ship's crew was allowed the freedom of Elizabethtown because the town lacked a jail. Eventually the sailors were taken to New York City and released. The cargo was sold.

The first of many rumors of an invasion of Elizabethtown was heard on February 10, 1776, when it was believed that General Sir Henry Clinton with the Royal Marines planned a raid from Staten Island for cattle. General William Livingston with 300 members of the militia hurried to the shore of the Arthur Kill to watch and wait. The British failed to appear. Two days later Colonel Nathaniel Heard and 700 volunteers were ordered to Staten Island to prevent a British landing and to repel foraging parties. Again no one appeared.

The lack of good maps of New Jersey was another one of General Washington's problems. He wrote to Congress requesting accurate maps and recommended that "gentlmen of known character be hired to make maps of roads, rivers, bridges, fords, mountains and passes." Robert Erskine, the manager of Ringwood Iron Mines, was selected to survey the area and map it. He prepared hundreds of maps They are considered the most accurate maps of New Jersey made during the Revolution. Erskine also developed the chain that was placed across the Hudson River to prevent British ships from sailing up it. Links for the chain were made at Ringwood. Pieces of the chain are still at Ringwood and on Constitution Island opposite the West Point Military Academy on the Hudson River.

Abraham Clark wrote to Colonel Elias Dayton on August 2, noting, "I feel the danger we are in. I am far from exulting in our imaginary happiness; nothing short of the almighty power of God can save us." Each signer of the Declaration of Independence knew that if the new nation failed to win the war, he faced a death sentence.

Clark was a sickly child who was considered too weak to become a farmer in Wheat Sheaf (Roselle). He was called "the poor man's lawyer" and was praised for being a mathematical genius. He, like most of the Elizabethtown men, was a member of the Presbyterian Church. He was buried, however, in the old cemetery in Rahway next to the Presbyterian Church there.

When he learned of the British arrival in New York Harbor, General Washington directed Livingston to remove all livestock from Staten Island and take it beyond First Mountain. Livingston also was placed in charge of the "Flying Camp," to guard the coastline between Amboy and Bergen Point. The "camp" was supposed to be composed of 10,000 men who could respond rapidly in any emergency. Unfortunately the quota was never reached and there were too few men to patrol the 19-mile long Arthur Kill from Elizabethtown to Amboy. There were even fewer men when the area to be defended was extended from Newark Bay through the Kill Van Kull to Paulus Hook (Jersey City).

Livingston also directed that the waterfront from Elizabethtown Point (at the mouth of the river) and Crane's Ferry (just east of the future Singer Manufacturing Company) be barricaded with fortifications. He ordered all ferrymen not to carry any individual over any creek or river who failed to produce a Continental passport or permission. Innkeepers also were prohibited from aiding any traveler, except officers, unless they displayed the necessary papers.

Soon after the British forces landed some of them assembled on the waterfront of the Arthur Kill only 500 feet from Elizabethtown Point. Two youths in a canoe paddled out and fired on them in what some believe were the first shots fired after independence was declared. Later in the day, the British asked the Staten Islanders to take an oath of allegiance to the crown, which they did.

On the evening of July 4, a British armed sloop with 14 guns ran near Elizabethtown Point and was attacked by the Continental militia on shore with the two 12-pounders. The sloop was set on fire and many men were killed.

Because the patriots in Elizabethtown anticipated an attack on the hamlet, many of them went beyond the Watchung Mountains to the homes of relatives and

Abraham Clark, "the poor man's lawyer," lived on a farm in Wheatsheaf (Roselle) and attended the Presbyterian Church in Elizabethtown. The only signer of the Declaration of Independence in New Jersey who lived north of the Raritan River, he opposed the Constitution until the Bill of Rights was adopted.

friends for safety or rented houses beyond the hamlet's limits. Mrs. Livingston and her children, for instance, joined her sister, the wife of Lord Stirling, in Basking Ridge. When the Livingstons returned home they discovered that Liberty Hall had been occupied by Continental soldiers who had done a great deal of damage. They refused to leave the house again, taking their chances with both armies. Livingston became the first state governor in August. Because he was a wanted man, he seldom returned to his home during the eight years of war. He made it a habit to move from place to place attempting to keep his location secret.

Flat boats were made at Elizabethport in anticipation of an invasion of Staten Island. Several attempts were made but were unsuccessful or only partially successful. In one, for instance, Lord Stirling learned the British were waiting for him despite his efforts to keep the pending raid a secret. In another by Colonel Elias Dayton and Colonel Matthias Ogden, they landed safely on Staten Island and captured 100 prisoners. Meanwhile Major General John Sullivan attacked north of Dayton and Ogden and was badly defeated. A retaliatory raid on Elizabethtown by the British followed within two weeks. The British went through Elizabethtown to Newark rounding up 400 head of cattle, 200 milk cows, and 400 sheep. The local militia fired at the raiders, but because there were too few militiamen, did not engage them in a major battle.

This statue of a minuteman was unveiled at Union Square on Elizabeth Avenue on July 4, 1906, marking the anniversary of the British attempt to capture the Continental army's supplies at Morristown in 1780.

After hostilities began, the British formed the New Jersey Volunteers, New Jersey residents who supported the Loyalists. One of these was Captain William Chandler, a physician and son of Reverend Thomas Bradbury Chandler and Mary E.B. Chandler. Critics of the British Army declare that the British failed to make good use of the Americans who supported them.

Reverend James Caldwell suggested that a cannon be placed at the gap above the Short Hills, also called Beacon Hill. The cannon known as the "Old Sow" would be fired three times and a large signal fire lighted to alert the militia if the enemy was observed approaching. The gap later was call Hobart's Gap for Episcopal Bishop John H. Hobart, who lived nearby. (Hobart College also was named for him.) There were 22 other lookouts along the Watchung Mountains from Orange County, New York to Bound Brook, including Great Notch off Rifle Camp Road in today's Little Falls, Eagle Rock in today's West Orange, Washington Rocks in South Orange and North Plainfield respectively, Beacon Hill, and at Tin Kettle Hill in Kenilworth. "Old Sow" is on view at Washington's Headquarters in Morristown.

Lord Stirling is credited with developing the beacons to be lighted when the British were observed approaching. Each beacon was a rough pyramid of logs filled with dry brush. The guard would light the brush, which could be seen for great distances, and fire the cannon three times every half hour to alert the militiamen. When the alert was over the guard removed the burned brush and filled it again. The beacons were easy to make, effective, and cheap.

The British ships continued to arrive from Nova Scotia until July 11, when more than 130 sails were counted and the British forces were estimated at 32,000 troops. Admiral Lord Richard Howe was in charge of the ships, and his brother Major General William Howe of the troops. At least 10,000 of them set up camp on Staten Island, while the rest were in New York. The people watching from the Jersey Shore and hills could observe the British soldiers in their red uniforms parading back and forth along the shore.

The British made their first raid for fresh food on Elizabethtown Point on July 10, 1776. Captain David Neill, who was in charge at Elizabethtown Point on July 4, fired on a British camp on Staten Island on August 26. The British returned fire. Captain Neill was killed on January 3, 1777, in the Battle of Princeton. Killed in the same battle was General Hugh Mercer, who was placed in charge of the Flying Camp after Livingston became governor on August 31.

General Washington put General Israel Putnam, the hero of Breed's Hill, in charge of the forces on Long Island. Thomas Morrell, a merchant who became a Methodist minister, called for volunteers and raised a company to fight in the Battle of Long Island, also known as the Battle of Brooklyn Heights, on August 27, 1776. General Putnam had the Continental forces guarded on three sides. The British attacked from the unguarded side, defeating the Continentals. Morrell's new company was literally cut to pieces, according to Theodore Thayer in *As We Were: The Story of Old Elizabethtown*. In the dead of night, General Washington with the help of Colonel John Grover's skilled fishermen-soldiers from Marblehead,

Massachusetts, carried about 9,000 Continental soldiers, horses, and equipment to Manhattan Island in their Durham boats. When sunrise came the British found their prey was gone. The British threatened Paulus Hook on September 23. It was ordered evacuated by the Continental forces and became the first place in New Jersey occupied by the British.

Washington realized that he would be unable to hold Manhattan Island, but he was determined not to give it up easily. He began moving toward White Plains. Enroute he built Fort Washington and Fort Lee opposite in New Jersey. After the Battle of White Plains on October 28, he turned toward the Hudson River, crossed it, and began his famous retreat across New Jersey.

When Fort Washington fell to the British on November 16, Washington ordered Fort Lee opposite it on the Hudson River evacuated at once. The soldiers fled without their arms, blankets, tents, supplies, and food. Their fires—with food cooking—were left burning. The British arrived a short time later and occupied their camp. The fleeing army crossed the Hackensack River at New Bridge and went by the home of Jan Zabriskie, a Tory. At the war's end, the house was confiscated and given to Baron Frederick Von Steuben, who trained the troops at Valley Forge during the war. Meanwhile the Continental Army continued to Acquackanonk Bridge (at today's Passaic) over the Passaic River, crossed, and burned it on November 21.

The next day the army reached Newark and camped from November 22 to 28, just north of the hamlet near present-day Branch Brook Park. It was during this stop that Washington met Thomas Paine, the British activist. Washington, discouraged by the defeats and the plight of his army, encouraged Paine to write something about the war. Paine composed *The Crisis*, which became a best seller. It began with the famous words:

> These are the times that try men's souls—the summer soldier and the sunshine patriot will, in this crisis, shrink from the service of his country, but he that stands now deserves the love and thanks of man and woman. Tyranny, like hell, is not easily conquered.

As Washington's troops marched out of Newark taking the Upper Road to Elizabethtown, the British and Hessian armies marched in taking the same camp site that the Continental troops had used. The American army passed the First Baptist Church of Lyon's Farms below Divident Hill and the Lyon's Farms Schoolhouse where the children lined up to cheer the troops. When the Redcoats appeared, the children hid in the woods. Some accounts state that the ground was covered with snow and that blood from the feet of the nearly shoeless soldiers turned the snow red.

The people of Elizabethtown were alarmed and those that could, moved beyond the Watchung Mountains. Those who stayed in their homes were subject to attacks by the enemy. Some families followed their soldier husband or father in the army after their houses were burned. They compounded Washington's problems for food, blankets, tents, and other supplies and slowed the army's progress. Washington ordered the women to travel in the rear of the troops.

The British left a contingent of soldiers in Newark and a larger one in Elizabethtown, which they occupied for nearly six weeks from November 29, 1776 until January 9, 1777, when the king's regiments were ordered to Amboy, a royal post, for most of the war. Philip Waldeck, a chaplain with the Third Waldeck Regiment of Hessian troops from Bremerlee, Germany, wrote in his diary that he thought the road to Elizabethtown was "an earthly paradise of cleared woods and beautiful orchards by the most fertile productive and richly cultivated land."

He was billeted in the home of a coopersmith, who was a Loyalist, while his wife was a rebel. Reverend Waldeck expressed surprise to find the house well-furnished with wallpaper on the walls. "I am amazed to find them so in a man of his class!" he wrote. While in Elizabethtown, he preached twice at St. John's and found the village "an agreeable place with sloops right in the middle of the city (on the Elizabeth River) and houses very much apart." But the occupation was an uneasy one for the British mercenaries. "The rebels attacked an outpost injurying three of His Majesty's men on December 11, 1776," and again on January 1, 1777.

British General Leslie landed at Elizabethtown Point on December 14 and camped at Elizabethtown until December 17 when he marched to Springfield, where the first battle of Springfield was fought. The two-hour engagement ceased when it got too dark to see the enemy. The American troops made camp expecting to continue the fight the next day. When dawn came, the Continental troops

General Washington passed the original Lyon's Farms schoolhouse in November 1776 during his retreat across New Jersey, and is said to have passed the building three more times. Burned during the Revolutionary War, it was rebuilt in 1784.

found that the enemy had disappeared in the darkness. Accounts vary concerning the number of men Leslie had. Some say he had only 600, others put the figure at 5,000. The British camped briefly at Spanktown (Rahway) on December 17, during the first Battle of Springfield.

The British general Lord William Howe offered the Americans a general amnesty if they would swear allegiance to the crown. Several residents of Elizabethtown met at the Arnet house on the site of the old Berkeley Carteret Hotel on East Jersey Street to discuss the offer and almost agreed to accept it. Hannah White Arnet, who was listening in the next room, burst into the room to oppose the men. When she stopped talking the men agreed that they would continue to support the Patriots. Mrs. Arnet is honored by two plaques in the First Presbyterian Cemetery on Broad Street.

During the retreat Washington ordered General Charles Lee to join him. Lee, who was in Basking Ridge, didn't move. As a result he was captured by the British and taken to New York City. He was a former British Army officer who believed he should be the commander-in-chief of the Continental Army. During the Battle of Monmouth on May 28, 1778, he retreated instead of attacking. General Horatio Gates also was a former British Army officer and like Lee believed that he should have been appointed commander-in-chief. He served through the war with honor.

Many Continental soldiers were engaged in a number of firefights. On Sunday, January 5, some militiamen went to Woodbridge to recover some 400 cattle and 200 sheep the British had stolen. The next day there was a two-hour long battle at Spanktown. On the same day General William Maxwell and the New Jersey militia were collecting salt. They were attacked by militant Highlanders and

Shepard Kollock was the founder, first editor, and publisher of The New Jersey Journal. *He moved the paper to Elizabethtown in 1785 and continued to operate it until he sold it in 1818.*

Hessians at the site of today's St. George Avenue and the Rahway River Park. General Maxwell and the British met in battle at Spanktown again on February 23. The British retreated to Perth Amboy.

Maxwell and the militia chased the rest of the Hessians out of Elizabethtown on January 8, retaking the hamlet. A skirmish took place in Bonhamtown (Edison) on January 16, 1777, while a foraging party raided farms near Springfield on February 1, and another foraging party met American troops at Quibbletown (New Market) a week later. The residents of Elizabethtown returned after General Maxwell drove the enemy out. They found their dwellings plundered, their gardens wasted, and their records destroyed. Some of them began burying their valuables in their yards. Others took them to relatives' homes beyond First and Second Mountains where they hoped they would be safe.

General Washington established his winter quarters in Morristown. Soldiers were quartered in many homes in the area partially to make it appear that there were more men than there actually were. He required all those persons who had taken oaths of allegiance to the British to surrender their papers and take oaths to the United States of America. Those who failed to do so were required to leave their farms and other possessions except their clothing and furniture and go to the enemy. Their cattle, horses, and wagons were ordered left behind, the notice said.

General Maxwell was in charge of troops in Elizabethtown, while General John Sullivan was in charge of those beyond First Mountain. They were kept busy moving from Elizabethtown to Scotch Plains, Chatham, and Springfield as foraging parties and British scouts entered the area. There were frequent skirmishes. Colonel Matthias Ogden was stationed in Elizabethtown proper.

In May 1777, Washington moved his troops to Middlebrook (Bound Brook) to watch the British in New Brunswick and Amboy from the Watchung Mountains. The British attempted to lure Washington out of the mountains, but he failed to budge. He wanted to avoid direct contact because of his poorly trained and small army. General Howe moved the British troops to New Brunswick as though he were enroute to capture Philadelphia. General Washington refused to leave his mountain. Howe moved his troops to an encampment between Millstone and Middlebush and built redoubts. Still Washington did not move. Howe returned to Amboy after plundering New Brunswick on June 22.

Patriotic banners were important. Before an official flag was adopted by Congress on June 14, 1777 with 13 stars and 13 stripes, several others had been developed and carried into battle. The first time the official flag was flown in battle may have been during the Battle of the Short Hills on June 26, 1777.

The British, who were tired of waiting for General Washington to bring his troops out of the safety of the mountains, began an invasion from Metuchen, Quibbletown, and Woodbridge on June 26, 1777. They attacked Lord Stirling at Metuchen. The British met the American troops at Oak Tree Pond in present day Edison. They continued to Ash Swamp, now Ash Brook Golf Course and Reservation in Scotch Plains. Near there General Lord Charles Cornwallis and General Sir William Howe, attracted by the odor of fresh-baked bread, asked

"Aunt" Betsy Frazee if they could have some of the bread she was baking. She answered that she would give it to them in fear, not love. Cornwallis refused the bread and ordered that nobody touch her or her house. All day long, the troops marched by the house and nobody bothered Aunt Betsy Frazee as she baked bread for the Continental soldiers. The house on Raritan and Terrill Roads became the home of the proprietors of the Terry-Lou Zoo after World War II and was operated for nearly 50 years. The Township of Scotch Plains now owns it and hopes to make a passive park out of the land. Historians hope to restore the house, which has changed little since the Revolution.

In October 1778, Catherine Smith, daughter of former mayor William Peartree Smith, (1774–1776) was married to Elisha Boudinot, younger brother of Elias, at the Belcher-Ogden Mansion in Elizabethtown. According to Lafayette, who was a wedding guest along with General Washington, Miss Smith sought to obtain a new gown in New York City for the wedding. Although she paid the money, the gown failed to arrive and she was married in her "old clothes," Lafayette said. The couple moved to Newark, where Elisha was a judge. Miss Smith apparently was attempting to participate in "London Trading," a name given for trading with the enemy or smuggling contraband into the hamlet. While common, it was prohibited by law. One of General Maxwell's duties was to prevent commerce between the Royalists and the Patriots.

The state legislature provided a bounty for persons who raised and sold wool, flax, and hemp. The export of wheat, beef, and livestock was prohibited. Workers who made paper were exempt from military service because of the need for paper.

General Washington was unhappy that Northern New Jersey lacked a newspaper. He called General Henry Knox and asked him to find somebody who could produce a paper for the patriotic cause. Knox did. Shepard Kollock of Elizabethtown was serving with the American forces at Morristown. Kollock agreed to publish the paper. The first issue of *The New Jersey Journal* was printed in Day's Inn (today the site of the Short Hills Mall, Millburn) on February 16, 1779. The next weekly issues were printed across the Passaic River in Chatham. Type was found on a tiny island in the Passaic River and it is believed that the newspaper may have been printed there at least once. Kollock moved the paper to New Brunswick at war's end and then to Elizabethtown in 1785.

British soldiers, led by General Thomas Stirling and guided by Elizabethtown's Loyalists such as Cornelius Hetfield Jr. and his cousin John Smith Hetfield, landed at Crane's Ferry with 1,000 men in February 1779. They crossed Woodruff's Farms north of the hamlet and marched to Liberty Hall in an attempt to capture Governor Livingston.

Henry Woodruff, whose farm was near the water, alerted General Maxwell, who was sleeping in a house in the center of the hamlet. Aaron Ogden, by then a major and aide-de-camp to General Maxwell, volunteered to see what was happening. As he approached the ferry, a man suddenly appeared in front of him and ordered him to halt. Major Ogden wheeled his horse and escaped to warn General Maxwell, but not before he was slashed with a bayonet.

The alarm was sounded and militiamen marched toward the village while the residents fled for the hills. Lieutenant Colonel Thomas Stirling arrived at Liberty Hall and demanded the governor's papers. Mrs. Livingston informed him that the governor was away. Susan Livingston, one of her daughters, is credited with grabbing a box of worthless correspondence and handing it to the officer.

The British continued into the village where they set the barracks, the blacksmith's shop, the Presbyterian parsonage, and the Elizabethtown Academy on fire. Mrs. Arnett and a Mrs. Egbert rolled away 26 barrels of flour before they could be destroyed in the academy where they were stored. The raiders also looted some homes and stole cattle. Colonels Matthias Ogden and Elias Dayton managed to seize the cattle before they were moved to Staten Island.

The British and Loyalists on another raid entered a tavern in Spanktown in June, capturing some soldiers who were drinking and eating there.

General "Mad Anthony" Wayne captured Stony Point in New York in July 1779. A cannon used by the British at Quebec City was seized and given to the people of Elizabethtown by Washington in appreciation for the Elizabethans' help in battle. Cast at Strasburg, Germany in 1758 for the French government, it was used in Canada in 1759. Captured by the British, it was used to kill General Richard Montgomery and wound Matthias Ogden and William Crane of Elizabethtown at Quebec City on December 31, 1775. It stands in front of the Union County Court House in Elizabeth.

Major "Light Horse" Henry Lee, father of Robert E. Lee, raided the British-held Paulus Hook and captured it. The Continental Army went into winter quarters at Morristown on December 1. Unlike the first encampment at Morristown, the soldiers were housed in log cabins at Jockey Hollow. The winter was the coldest of the war and the men were without fuel, wood, clothes, blankets, decent shoes or boots, and food. Elizabethtown was occupied during much of the winter by its own troops.

The militia raided Staten Island on January 14 and 15, 1780. They were told to take only livestock, horses, wagons, and items of military value. They took anything they could find. They fled when they realized that the enemy had been warned. A garrison of 60 men from Elizabethtown was captured.

On January 25, 1780, the British, led by Cornelius Hatfield Jr., raided both Elizabethtown and Newark. Presbyterian churches in both hamlets were destroyed. Also burned were the courthouses in Elizabethtown and Newark Academy. Some houses in both hamlets were burned after they had been searched for valuables. Cornelius's father, a deacon in the Elizabethtown church, provided his red store house for the church so services could continue in Elizabethtown.

The British still wanted to capture the American armaments and stores at Morristown. General Wilhelm von Knyphausen landed at DeHart's Point, a short distance west of the old Singer plant in Elizabethtown, with British and Hessian troops on June 6, 1780 and began to march toward Morristown. General von Knyphausen believed that the American forces at Morristown would surrender easily because he had received reports of mutinies and desertions. He planned to seize prisoners, too.

Governor James Robertson of New York wrote that 6,000 men landed at Elizabethtown Point and others at Crane's Ferry. They waited for the second embarcation by return boats Then they began to move in order to surprise General Maxwell's brigade. They planned to march to the Short Hills (Millburn) and wait for a third group of soldiers before pushing on toward Morristown. The march began from Elizabethtown Point toward the Courthouse and from Crane's Ferry up New Point Road to the Crossroads and the Courthouse.

Colonel Elias Dayton, quartered at the barracks, sent a guard of 12 men to the Crossroads (Elizabeth Avenue and Division Street) to delay the invaders until an express rider could alert the sentry by "Old Sow" and sound the alarm. The guard was led by 19-year-old Moses Ogden. They fired at the British at close range and then withdrew quickly. One of the bullets struck General Thomas Stirling, the British commander. The British troops stopped while the general, who was knocked off his horse, was carried from the scene. General von Knyphausen took his place at the head of the column. This incident is known as the Battle of Elizabethtown.

An eyewitness to the march termed it one of the most beautiful he had ever seen. There were the Queen's Rangers with drawn swords and glittering helmets flashing in the sunlight as they rode on carefully groomed horses, followed by the infantry on foot, all clad in new red or green uniforms. The march took the British along what is now Broad Street and West Jersey Street in Elizabeth. Meanwhile Old Sow at the gap on the heights above Springfield was booming three times every half hour calling militiamen to assemble.

This small painting of Hannah Ogden Caldwell (left) is in the museum of the First Presbyterian Church. Her murder by a British soldier is shown incorrectly on the Union County seal (above), the only seal in the country depicting a murder.

Militiamen hurried to Connecticut Farms to join the battle. Sixty militiamen halted the British and Hessian soldiers briefly at the West Branch of the Elizabeth River. General Maxwell and his brigade drove the enemy back. One of the enemy shot Mrs. Hannah Ogden Caldwell, wife of Reverend James Caldwell, as she sat in the parsonage with two of her young children, a serving woman, and a young girl of about 14 years. Her body was carried to the Wade house by friends before the parsonage was burned. The wanton, unnecessary murder on June 7, 1780 was investigated by the American forces, who were inflamed by it. The murder is depicted on the Union County seal, which is the only seal in the nation that shows such a scene. Some people believed that it occurred because of Reverend Caldwell's talks against the crown.

Washington advanced to Springfield while Colonel Dayton and his men at the Rahway River prevented the British from continuing their march to Morristown. Young Moses Ogden was killed in the action that day. At first Knyphausen made camp in Connecticut Farms, then decided to return to Elizabethtown Point and wait for reinforcements from General Sir Henry Clinton. When the soldiers realized that they were not going on to Morristown, many of them forced entry into the houses and stole the valuables. They also removed jewelry and money from the dead bodies. When they finished they set fire to the church and most of the houses and outbuildings. A heavy rain with much thunder and lightning drenched the beautiful soldiers' uniforms before they were able to erect their tents for the night.

A few of them found some of the famous "Jersey Lightning" (hard cider), drank it, and forced their way into Liberty Hall when they reached it. As they entered, there was a bright flash of light on the hall stairs where Catherine, one of Governor Livingston's daughters, stood in her long white nightgown. The drunken soldiers saw her, and believing she was Mrs. Caldwell's ghost, fled from the mansion. Instead of continuing over the bridge of boats to Staten Island, General von Knyphausen directed that the men pitch their tents at Elizabethtown Point. They camped there from June 8 to June 23, when they attempted to seize Morristown again.

The German and British dead in Connecticut Farms were buried in an unmarked grave in the Connecticut Farms Presbyterian Church Cemetery. When an education building was added to the church in the 1940s, the graves were moved to the other side of the church opposite the Connecticut Farms School. A memorial stone was placed on the site in July 2001 by representatives of American and Canadian patriotic groups.

Washington, who used the church as his headquarters on June 8, 1780, directed General Edward Hand to harass the British camp. Hand's forces made one strong attack that nearly overpowered von Knyphausen's camp. The rest of the time he made little forays on the camp. Fighting extended from the Arthur Kill to the Stone Bridge. British and Hessian soldiers looted many of the dwellings along the river, including the Belcher House. Mr. and Mrs. William Peartree Smith moved to their daughter's home in Newark. Mosquitoes added to the discomfort of both armies.

During the Battle of Springfield on June 23, 1780, Reverend James Caldwell, "the fighting pastor," gave out hymnals by Isaac Watts to the Continental soldiers saying, "Give 'em Watts, boys! Give 'em Watts!" The torn out pages from the hymnals were used as wadding for their guns.

Washington put General Nathanael Greene in charge of any further battles on the road to Morristown. The wait finally ended when British General Sir Henry Clinton arrived at the Point and the second attempt to reach Morristown began early on June 23. The soldiers followed the same route that they had more than two weeks earlier. Just before they arrived at the Rahway River at the Springfield line half of the troops turned off the road to take Vauxhall Road. Continental troops were waiting for them at the bridges over the Rahway River's East Branch at Vauxhall road and main branch at Morris Avenue. The bridge decks had been removed so they had to wade through the water. The bridge on Vauxhall Road was called Little's Bridge.

Fighting was fierce at both bridges. Most of the militia was in the hills under General Maxwell and General John Stark behind the battlefield to prevent the enemy from penetrating the hills. All roads were clogged with soldiers and militiamen. The enemy troops crossed the East Branch of the Rahway River into today's Millburn and part of Maplewood. At that time it was all part of Springfield. "Light Horse" Harry Lee and Colonel Matthias Ogden also went to the heights near the hill in the rear of the village. Colonel Elias Dayton and Colonel Israel Angell were at the first bridge on Morris Avenue over the Rahway River. They waited on the Springfield side of the bridge after the bridge's planks were removed. When the enemy soldiers appeared they had to wade through the river and at the same time face the fire from the American troops. Colonel Israel Shreve was placed a half mile in back of them at the second bridge over Van Winkle's Creek. The planks had been removed from the bridge here also and the enemy would have to wade a second time. It was during this battle that Reverend James Caldwell went into the Presbyterian Church and picked up an armful of hymnals by Reverend Isaac Watts of England, ripped out the pages, and handed them to the soldiers, urging them to "Give 'em Watts boys! Give them Watts!" The paper was used for wadding in their rifles.

The fighting at the first bridge lasted some two hours and at the second bridge about 40 minutes. The battle at Little's Bridge was spirited. The enemy army finally forded the river and headed for the gap. All day more and more militiamen joined the others. The American forces gathered around the gap and on the ridge of the Short Hills (Beacon Hill). Instead of pressing forward, up the mountain and through the gap, the British and Hessian soldiers retreated back to Elizabethtown Point. As they left the spring fields they set fire to 19 of 23 houses and the Presbyterian Church. Instead of camping at the Arthur Kill, they crossed to Staten Island on their bridge of boats. It was the last major conflict in the North. During the battle the home of Dr. Jonathan Dayton on Morris Avenue was struck by a cannonball and was named the Cannonball House. It apparently was spared from destruction because the British and Hessians used it as a hospital. The Springfield Historical Society has operated it since the early 1950s.

A pair of brothers with the Hessian troops at the Battle of Springfield deserted during the fighting near Little's Bridge. They hid in a house in Millburn now called the Hessian House. After the war they settled on land in the hamlet and according to legend became good American citizens. Many of the mercenaries deserted. Some of them went to the Ramapo Mountains where they intermarried with the Native Americans and African Americans and became the Jackson Whites. Efforts by their descendants to be recognized as a Native-American tribe have so far failed.

A story is told about a boy with a homemade drum who came alone to the field of battle. A soldier, thinking the boy was the drummer boy who tapped the commands on the drum, called to him to go forward. The boy did and was killed. He was never identified.

Although there were no more battles, there were many skirmishes among the patriots and the enemy. Both foraged for food and stole farmers' produce, firewood, apple jack, and animals. The people of the Elizabethtown area and their possessions were not safe. Few dwellings were untouched by vandals. There were frequent small skirmishes in both Elizabethtown and Staten Island between the opposing armies.

The day after the British returned to Staten Island, General Philemon Dickinson and a detachment of militia destroyed the fortifications the British had built along the Arthur Kill. Colonel Matthias Ogden and Captain Jonathan Dayton were taken prisoner on November 8, 1780, as they slept at the home of

William Herd in Connecticut Farms. They were taken to New York City, where they were allowed to walk freely on the streets. Ogden became very popular with the British officers and was invited to eat with them. One night one of them made a toast to the "damnation of all rebels," according to Theodore Thayer in *As We Were*. Ogden surprised everybody by throwing the wine in his glass in the officer's face. The officers at the table are said to have apologized to Ogden. Ogden later made an effort to capture Prince William of England, who came to New York to see the fighting, but he was unable to reach the future king. Ogden was exchanged in time to participate in the Battle of Yorktown.

Meanwhile Washington was negotiating with the French. It was decided that the French Army would march from Newport, Rhode Island while the navy would sail to Virginia. In an effort to fool the British, Washington directed that bake ovens be built along the Passaic River in Chatham to make French bread. The French Army began to march. The people in Connecticut, New York, and New Jersey lined the roads to see the soldiers in their handsome uniforms. They were praised for their good behavior. British spies watched and tried to guess where they were going. They marched through Springfield, but failed to stop at the ovens. They continued onward. The British expected them to turn back toward New York City but when they passed Trenton, they realized that New York was not the target.

They traveled on to Virginia, where they defeated the British at Williamsburg and Yorktown. The British surrendered on October 19, 1781. Sentinels were posted along the streets of Elizabethtown and called out to each passerby to account for himself. David Woodruff and Philip McCrea were walking in the town one night and were hailed by the sentinel. They failed to answer. The sentinel fired and killed McCrea.

Reverend James Caldwell became a victim of martial law when he went to Elizabethtownport to meet Miss Beulah Murray, who was arriving on the ferry from New York City under a flag of truce. She was the daughter of one of the Quakers who attempted to smuggle banned goods from the *Beulah* into Elizabethtown. The ferry had already docked when Reverend Caldwell arrived on November 24, 1781. He went aboard the ferry in search of a package she said she had left aboard it. He was challenged by the sentry as he left the boat and failed to stop. The young sentry shot and killed him. Reverend Caldwell's body was carried to the steps of Boxwood Hall. Elias Boudinot, a lawyer, placed each of the Caldwell children with families in Elizabethtown. One was taken to France by Lafayette but later returned to the United States.

The soldier, James Morgan, was seized and charged with murder. He was tried in the Presbyterian Church in the west fields (Westfield) and found guilty. He was sentenced to be hanged on Gallows Hill, sometimes called Morgan's Hill, in the west fields. Many stories grew from the death. Morgan, a native of Ireland, was charged with being a Papist in the pay of the British. A few pointed out that he was a sentry doing his duty, who was new to the community and didn't know Reverend Caldwell.

Marquis de Lafayette is said to have danced on the lawn of The Carteret Arms, an inn near the Stone Bridge. After 1837, the building was used for a variety of purposes.

Captain William C. DeHart, an aide-de-camp to General Winfield Scott during the War of 1812 and the Mexican War and grandson of John DeHart, the former mayor, wrote an article stating that Caldwell's death was probably an accident. He noted that as a stranger, Morgan didn't know Reverend Caldwell. Morgan was following orders. His article was criticized by the people and DeHart lost his popularity in town because Pastor Caldwell's popularity continued long after his death.

Although the war wasn't over, many of the Loyalists began leaving New York City on January 1, 1782. Hostilities continued. On March 15, 1782, a ship flying a flag of truce and carrying a Hessian paymaster was boarded at Shooter's Island by masked men believed to be Refugees (Tories) who stole money plus valuables from some of the passengers. Peace talks began in Paris on April 12, 1782. On March 3, 1783, Major William Crane, later a general, captured the armed ship *Eagle* and the sloop *Katy* within pistol shot of the Battery in New York City. The *Eagle* had to be left because she was grounded. The *Katy* was brought to Elizabethtown where the cargo and vessel were sold at auction. Crane was elevated to brigadier general for this action.

The Continental Army moved up to the West Windsor Cantonment at Vail's Gate, New York, where New York City could be watched while the peace treaty was being negotiated. The army was there for more than a year. One day Colonel Francis Barber was killed by a falling tree being chopped down by some soldiers.

Barber, the former teacher at the Elizabethtown Academy, was known for being a strict disciplinarian. Some people claimed the tree was cut down on purpose because most of the soldiers were experienced woodsmen, according to E. Jane Townsend, former site manager at the cantonment. Others said it was an accident.

Colonel Matthias Ogden visited France in 1783 and brought home the news that the Treaty of Paris was signed, the war was ended, and the United States was a new nation. Elias Boudinot, who was elected president of the Continental Congress on November 4, 1782, received notice of the official ending of the war on November 1, 1783. He declared a day of Thanksgiving, which some people claim was the nation's first Thanksgiving Day. Later he urged President George Washington to designate a Thanksgiving Day and he did. The British troops finally evacuated New York City on November 25, 1783, called Evacuation Day.

Property of known Tories was confiscated by the new government. Some of the Tories went to England where they were offered small pensions but were not accepted by the English society. Some went to Nova Scotia or New Brunswick, Canada, where they were well treated and accepted, but received no money. A few like Reverend Chandler were able to return to or stayed in New Jersey. James Ricketts, a Livingston relative, returned to the family farm in the meadows and was undisturbed. He joined the Royal Americans (Tories) during the war, but fought in the West Indies. Cavalier Jouet returned twice but was not accepted. Two of his grandchildren, who were born in Canada, moved to the Roselle area when adults. Cornelius Hatfield Jr., the Loyalist who torched the Presbyterian Church and the Academy, returned to claim his father's estate. He returned to England. He was not tried because of the terms of the peace treaty.

George Washington was elected as the first president of the United States on February 4, 1789. He began his eight day journey to New York City on April 16 for his first inauguration. He rode by coach between hamlets but just before entering a village, he mounted his white horse. He was greeted at each community by its leading citizens and escorted into town by the militia and light horse. The roads were lined with cheering people. Pretty girls threw flowers in his path. Leading citizens of each community and Revolutionary War veterans greeted him.

President-elect Washington spent the night of April 22 in Woodbridge, then stopped at a tavern in Rahway to greet the people in the morning. He continued to Elizabethtown, where he stopped first at the Red Lion Tavern on the site of the Elizabeth Public Library and then continued to Boxwood Hall, the home of Elias Boudinot, for a banquet. Guests included Henry Knox, John Jay, Governor William Livingston, Richard Henry Lee, Charles Carroll, John Langdon, and community leaders. After he ate, the President-elect was escorted to the Arthur Kill to a decorated barge manned by 13 sailors dressed in white smocks and black-fringed caps for the trip to Murray's Wharf at the foot of Wall Street. Thirteen young girls, one for each state, were at the dock to see him off on the barge. Six more barges carrying dignitaries accompanied the ceremonial barge to New York. Washington walked through the crowd to the Franklin House, where he lived while in New York City.

Washington, seated on his white horse, listens to the Declaration of Independence being read to his troops on July 9, 1776.

Martha Washington meanwhile traveled by carriage with an escort from Mount Vernon. She spent one night at Liberty Hall as the guest of Governor and Mrs. William Livingston. The next day she continued her journey by carriage and crossed to the Battery by ferry. The first inauguration was at Federal Hall in New York City on April 30, 1789. Senate Chamber Chancellor Robert Livingston administered the oath of office to Washington.

Visitors were frequent at Liberty Hall in Elizabethtown. In addition to John Jay, husband of Sarah Livingston, the governor's oldest daughter, there was Judge John Cleves Symmes, a land speculator, who married Susan Livingston, a daughter of the governor. Judge Symmes was successful in interesting many of the gentlemen of Elizabethtown in investing in land in Ohio. His daughter Ann eloped with the future president William Henry Harrison, according to tradition, by climbing out a window at Liberty Hall.

Chevalier D'Anterroches, a Lafayette relative, favored the crown when the war broke out. Captured as he fought with the British, he was taken to Chatham where he met and married Mary Vanderpool. They built a house on a farm on the road to Rahway and became leaders in the community.

Meanwhile the people were rebuilding the Academy, the courthouse, their houses, barns, and sheds, replanting trees, vegetables, and flower gardens, restocking their fowl, cows, pigs, and sheep, and replacing their fences. The men joined road crews either to repair the road in front of their own property or in the hamlet in general. Stores were rebuilt, repaired, and restocked.

Churches in most cases were rebuilt within the walls of those that were destroyed. The Presbyterian Church was rebuilt. St. John's Episcopal Church, which for a while was the only church in Elizabethtown, was badly damaged because it was used as a stable, quarters for troops, and a warehouse. Efforts were made to burn it at least twice. The pipes of the organ were removed and melted down for bullets. The tombstones in the adjacent graveyard were used for fireplaces to cook food or to keep warm and as tables. A baptismal font donated to the church by Cavalier Jouet before the war and hidden throughout the war was returned to the church, where it continues to be used today. Money for the restoration of the churches and Academy was raised by holding lotteries on Shooter's Island. The churches frowned on the prohibited lotteries, but willingly accepted the money to rebuild. Reverend Uzal Ogden, a cousin of Mrs. James Caldwell, served St. John's Church during some of Reverend Thomas B. Chandler's illnesses.

One new religious denomination began at this time, the Methodist Episcopal Church. It was brought to the community by a Mrs. Jonathan Morrell, whose son Thomas became a Methodist minister. He was a circuit rider for ten years before he opened a meetinghouse near Adelphian Academy on Water Street. He conducted services there for 34 years near the present Morrell Street, which was named for him.

In June 1782, Reverend James Francis Armstrong became the supply pastor for 18 months at the Presbyterian Church. The rebuilt church was dedicated January 1, 1786. Shortly afterward Reverend William Adolphus Linn was called to become pastor. He stayed only four months and was replaced by Reverend David Austin, who published two magazines, one religious and the other dealing with farming. He became involved with the millennium movement and in May 1796 said Christ would return to establish his kingdom on earth. All day long young ladies dressed in white and other members of the congregation sat and waited. The day ended and nobody came. A group of trustees asked the Presbytery to dismiss him. It finally did. He was followed by Reverend John Giles, who served as pastor for about a year starting on June 24, 1800.

Reverend Dr. Chandler also was assisted by Reverend Samuel Spraggs because of his illnesses. Reverend Spraggs died in 1784. Reverend Menzies Rayner was called as priest for the Episcopal church in 1795 and served six years. He was followed by Reverend Frederick Beasley, a classmate at the College of New Jersey of Reverend Henry Kollock, pastor at the First Presbyterian Church and a son of Shepard Kollock, founder of the *New Jersey Journal*. Their service was brief. Reverend Beasley's was less than a year and Reverend Kollock's three years.

There were no wartime mayors in Elizabethtown. Post-war mayors included Stephen Crane, 1788–1789, who was reelected after the hamlet was chartered by the State Legislature; John DeHart, 1789–1795; and Elias Dayton, 1795–1805.

Although the population of Elizabethtown was small, estimated at only 1,200 people, it had several outstanding citizens. The Reverend James Caldwell had the distinction of being the first person in Elizabethtown to have a monument dedicated to him. It was dedicated in the Presbyterian Church cemetery on Broad Street on November 24, 1845, by the Sons of Cincinnati. Reverend James Caldwell was pastor of the church from 1762 to 1776, when the family fled to New Providence. The family later moved to the vacant parsonage in Union Township. The inscription on the Caldwell monument states:

> James Caldwell Born in Charlotte County Virginia April 1734, Graduated from Princeton 1759, Ordained the pastor of the First Presbyterian Church of Elizabethtown 1762. After serving as Chaplain in the Army of the Revolution and acting as commissary to the troops in New Jersey, He was killed by a shot from a sentinel at the Elizabethtown Port November 24, 1781.

Reverend Caldwell made frequent home visits to members of his congregation. He urged all the African Americans in the area to attend the church and welcomed them when they did. Reverend Caldwell and his wife Hannah had nine children. Mrs. Caldwell was encouraged to leave the Connecticut Farms parsonage in June 1780, but she believed that as a woman she would be safe.

A 22-foot obelisk monument was dedicated to Abraham Clark three years later in the old Rahway Cemetery by the citizens of Rahway. The Daughters of the American Revolution put an upright sandstone marker on his grave in 1924. A bronze plaque was placed on the front in 1968.

This cannon was given to the people of Elizabethtown by George Washington in appreciation for their support during the war for independence. Cast in 1758, it was used by the French and later the British to defend Quebec and was eventually seized at Stony Point by General Anthony Wayne. It was unveiled in 1905.

Francis Barber, the teacher at the Academy, followed his students to war and participated in many of the engagements including Mohawk Valley with Colonel Dayton, the attack on the Indians in Wyoming Valley, and the Battles of Connecticut Farms, Springfield, and Yorktown. He married twice: to Mary Ogden, sister of Matthias and Aaron; and after she died at 21, her cousin Nancy Ogden. He resided in the Bonnell house on East Jersey Street, considered to be the oldest dwelling still standing in Elizabeth. It was restored in the 1960s by the Elizabethtown Historical Foundation.

Elias Dayton became a brigadier general when William Maxwell resigned. As such, General Dayton was the highest ranking officer in New Jersey at war's end. A native of Elizabethtown, he operated a store on Broad Street just above his dock on the Elizabethtown River near the Stone Bridge. He had a fleet of boats that traded along the coast, in the Caribbean, and occasionally with Europe. He was a veteran of the French and Indian Wars in 1764, when the British attacked Native Americans near Detroit. During this period a fort was built and named for him in New York. He was commissioned a colonel of the 3rd Regiment of New Jersey Regulars in February 1776 and served through the war. Three horses were shot from under him in battle. He participated in the Battles of Brandywine, Germantown, Monmouth, Connecticut Farms, Springfield, and Yorktown, the Western Exposition under General Sullivan, and the guarding of Elizabethtown. He was promoted to major general of the 2nd Division of the New Jersey Militia in June 1793.

Elias Boudinot is considered by some historians to have been the first president of the United States since he was president of the Continental Congress when the Treaty of Paris was signed, signalling the official creation of the new nation.

In addition to operating Elias Dayton & Son, he served in the New Jersey State Legislature and as president and member of the Board of Trustees of the Presbyterian Church. He was the first president of the New Jersey Society of Cincinnati, suggested by General Henry Knox. The society, named for a Roman general, was composed of men and their oldest sons who served as officers in the Revolution. Membership today continues to be by primogeniture, the eldest son of the descendant of the Revolutionary War veteran. George Washington was the first national president. In 1790, the hamlet of Losantiville on the Ohio River, established by John Cleves Symmes, was renamed Cincinnati to honor the society.

Elias Boudinot IV, president of the Continental Congress when the Treaty of Paris was signed ending the war, was a lawyer. He studied law with Richard Stockton of Princeton and married Stockton's sister Hannah while Stockton married his sister Annis, a poet. He served as president of the Board of Trustees of the Presbyterian Church and was appointed Commissary General of Prisoners when the war began. He served in the Continental Congress from 1778 to 1783. In 1785, he was appointed superintendent of the United States Mint in Philadelphia. He gave a pair of crystal chandeliers to the Presbyterian church as a farewell gift. They survived a fire in 1944 and a tornado in 1889. They continue to hang in the church.

Although he retired to Burlington to live with his only daughter, Susan Vergereau Bradford, in 1795, he was elected to the board of trustees of the College of New Jersey (Princeton University) and founded its Cabinet of Natural History. He was a member of the American Board of Commissioners for Foreign Missions. He also was founder and first president of the American Bible Society, which continues to exist. Boudinot suggested that Elizabethtown be the capital of New Jersey as it had been, but Trenton was selected because it was closer to the people in the southern part of the state. He and others in the hamlet also sought to have Elizabethtown made the nation's capitol. Again the national legislators wanted a spot closer to the southern part of the country.

Matthias Ogden sought adventure and found it. He was with Aaron Burr Jr. on the long trek through the Maine woods and marshes to the St. Lawrence River in an effort to capture Canada. He married Colonel Dayton's daughter Hannah on his return home. He joined General Philip Schuyler in the Mohawk Valley in 1776 with his father-in-law to fight British, Tories, and Indians. When he returned home he was assigned to the heights above Middlebrook until he was sent to Newark to guard it from a British attack. He went to France when hostilities ceased, to suggest a business arrangement with the French. He was awarded the Le droit du Tabouret for his service in the war by King Louis XVI, but failed to reach any business agreement. He brought word of the signing of the Treaty of Paris ending the war when he returned home. He resumed his study of law. He was involved in land speculation in the West with other Elizabethans, acquired a contract to carry mail between New York and Philadelphia by stage coach, and had a contract to mint coins. He also operated the family tannery with his brother-in-law Oliver Spencer. In 1791, he died of yellow fever.

Matthias's brother Aaron Ogden became governor in 1812 because he opposed the War of 1812. He both attended and taught at the old Academy, was a graduate of the College of New Jersey, and became a lawyer. He fought in the Battles of Connecticut Farms and Springfield. He was unable to negotiate a prisoner exchange of John Andre for Benedict Arnold to save Andre's life as ordered by General Washington.

In 1798, when a war with France threatened, Aaron Ogden was promoted to lieutenant colonel by Governor Richard Howell, who formed the 11th Infantry Regiment. He was camped in Scotch Plains with the 12th New York Regiment. Together they were called the Union Brigade. Aaron Ogden was deputy quartermaster general and second in command. He was elected to the U.S. Senate in 1801.

Jonathan Dayton was elected to the state legislature and served as its speaker from 1794 to 1799. He also was a U.S. senator from 1799 to 1805, and was promoted to the rank of brigadier general by President John Adams. Dayton was also in the House of Representatives for eight years and served one term as speaker.

John DeHart, twice mayor of Elizabethtown, was a well-known lawyer who had a pleasant house. He was a member of the Essex County Committee of Correspondence and attended the Continental Congresses. His daughter Abigail married Colonel John Mayo, who purchased a house on East Jersey Street as his summer home. Mayo's daughter Maria married General Winfield Scott who made the house his home.

The park nearby is named Scott Park. Edward J. Grassmann built a duplicate of the Scott house on Westminster Avenue in 1960s. The original house was razed about 1928 for a gas station. The park area was known as "Horse Hollow" and had a small stream to the Elizabeth River running through it.

The French Revolution caused an exodus of nobility from France and of those who associated with nobility. One hundred and twenty refugees arrived in Elizabethtown, where there already was a French presence. Some were well-to-do and purchased large homes and entertained lavishly. Others taught piano, dancing, and French language classes. Some were painters and did portraits, especially of the young ladies in the town. A few opened stores. Although many returned to France when it appeared to be safe, a large group continued to reside in Elizabethtown.

The idea of freedom spread to the various neighborhoods. Small hamlets began to separate from Elizabethtown. The first of these were Springfield and Westfield in 1793 and 1794, respectively. The people did not desire to be called for jury duty when they had little interest in the cases.

During the Revolutionary War, New Jersey issued paper currency that was declared "Not Worth A Continental" because it had little gold or silver to back it and people refused to accept it. Coins that were used were usually Spanish or British. Walter Mould, Thomas Goadsby, and Albion Cox suggested to the General Assembly that coins could be minted for the new state. The legislature approved the opening of a mint on June 1, 1788. The three men were authorized to coin £3 million. Each coin was 6 penny weights and 6 grams. The first mint was beside the Rahway River on the site of the former Huffman-Koos furniture store in Rahway. The coins featured a drawing of a horsehead and a plow and the Latin words, "Nova Caesarea" for New Jersey. The reverse side featured a large shield and the Latin, "E Pluribus Unum," meaning from many, one. It is believed that it was the first time the words were used on coins in this country. Matthias Ogden established a mint in Elizabethtown and Mould, one of the original partners, moved to Morristown to start another mint.

After Governor Livingston died in 1790, Liberty Hall was occupied by his daughter Susanna and her husband Judge John Cleves Symmes. In 1798, Henry Brockholst Livingston sold the mansion to Lord Bolingbroke, an Englishman, who resided in the house until 1806, when he returned to England. It was purchased by Governor Livingston's niece, Susan Livingston Kean Niemcewicz, who was living in Elizabeth with her son Peter Kean. Susan's first husband, John Kean of Charleston, South Carolina, had died young. She hired Count Julian Ursyn Niemcewicz as a tutor for Peter and subsequently married him. Peter changed the name of the estate to Ursino in honor of the count for his estates in Poland.

By 1800, the people of Elizabethtown had settled down to live their lives, farm their farms, pursue their interests, and worship their God. The years they had suffered in the Revolution were behind them. They had endured a shake-down cruise in the formation of a new nation. Their thoughts turned westward to the great expanse of land waiting to be developed.

3. A NEW CITY AND COUNTY 1800–1857

In the period from 1800 to 1857, when Union County separated from Essex County after 189 years, the hamlet was transformed from a collection of neat colonial farms occupied by people who seldom ventured 10 miles from their homes to one in which people could travel rapidly by train to distance places.

There were still excellent craftsmen such as Aaron Miller and David Ross, both bellsmiths; Aaron Lane, Matthew and Benjamin Halsted, silversmiths; Isaac Brokaw, his son John, and Kennedy Miller, clockmakers; Aaron Hatfeld and Richardson Gray, cabinetmakers; Elias Wade, Moses Chandler, and Joseph C. Wade, makers of wagons and carriages, and men like Daniel Day, John Stevens, and Alfred Vail who sought faster and more efficient ways to produce products.

Shepard Kollock began to print books as well as the *New Jersey Journal* in Elizabethtown. Among them was an almanac. He also served as a judge of the Court of Common Pleas for Essex County for 35 years and in 1822, he sold the newspaper and became postmaster of Elizabethtown. He held the post until 1829.

The post office started in 1775 in Elizabethtown. Since there was no delivery, a person anticipating mail would have to visit the store or inn designated as the post office. The names of persons who had mail were listed in the *New Jersey Journal*. Prices of sending a letter varied, depending upon both distance and weight.

The success of the Philadelphia-Lancaster Turnpike, a toll road, built in 1792–1794, 62 miles between Philadelphia and Lancaster, Pennsylvania, encouraged the formation of turnpike companies. One of several of these in the Essex County area of New Jersey was on the old road from Morristown to Elizabethtown, chartered in 1801 and opened in 1804. Pikes were placed across the roadway at places where the tolls were collected. Different fees were charged for each pedestrian, horse, cow, sheep, wagon, or carriage. Soon "shunpikes" grew up around the toll gates. These were unofficial roads that went around the pikes and were used by people who wanted to avoid paying the toll. Two of them still exist today as regular streets in Springfield and Chatham. At Springfield, the turnpike branched off toward Newark and became the Newark-Springfield Turnpike and then Springfield Avenue. It diverted the traffic toward Newark, where much progress was made to improve transportation. Newark grew faster than Elizabethtown and became the third city in the nation in 1836. Elizabethtown waited until 1855 to become a city.

The Adelphian Academy, a private school, was built on Water Street (Elizabeth Avenue) at today's Scott Place in 1806 by a group of stockholders who were mostly Elizabethtown residents. Several other private schools also were organized for a few years each. The one-room North End School built just before the Revolutionary War on land provided by David Lyon beside Brackett's Brook and the Road to Newark (Salem Park) was quasi-private. Funds to pay the teacher were raised by subscriptions until the 1840s, when it became a public school.

Aaron Burr Jr. and Alexander Hamilton both attended the old Academy in Elizabethtown but not at the same time. Historians do not know when they met. They were both active in the Revolutionary War and later in politics, with Burr finally killing Hamilton in a famous duel on July 11, 1804.

It soon became apparent during this time that Essex County needed a new courthouse. The residents of Newark wanted to keep the courthouse in Newark, but the people in Elizabethtown wanted the courthouse closer to them and the people in other parts of the county wanted it west of Newark. Finally the state legislature adopted a law setting the second Tuesday and Wednesday of February 1807 for an election on the proposed site. Originally 11 spots were nominated. By February, they were narrowed to Newark and Day's Hill in Camptown (Chancellor Avenue, Irvington). This election is called the most crooked election

Aaron Burr Jr. (left) and Alexander Hamilton (right) both attended the Elizabethtown Academy. Burr later shot and killed Hamilton in a famous 1804 duel.

in the area's history. Everybody voted: white men, African-American men, women, and even the people in the cemeteries all voted several times. In the end Newark was selected.

The courthouse in Elizabethtown was for municipal cases only. The 11-year-old building that replaced the one that burned during the Revolution was destroyed by fire on April 26, 1808. It was partially rebuilt a second time and put in use in 1810–1811, but the building went unfinished for many years.

Under the 1776 state constitution, the vote was granted to all people as long as they had £50. There was much criticism of the 1807 election, and Moses Miller Crane of Elizabethtown, who is called the "Father of Union County" was determined that African Americans and women would not vote again. He encouraged opposition to their voting. A law was adopted eliminating the poll tax and granting all men the right to vote. The 15th Amendment to the U.S. Constitution in 1870 granted suffrage to all males over 21 years of age in the United States and its territories. Women still had to wait until 1920 to gain the vote.

The fight for independence from the mother country in the eighteenth century extended to independence for small outlying communities in Elizabethtown as the area began to splinter into more boroughs and townships. Rahway Township was created in 1804, Union Township was formed in 1808, and New Providence in 1809. Union Township contained part of Lyon's Farms, whose merchants gave their addresses as Elizabethtown.

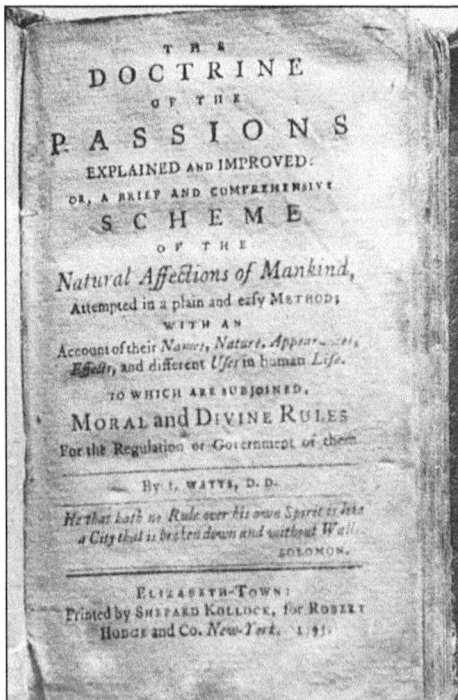

In addition to printing and editing The New Jersey Journal, *Shepard Kollock also did job printing such as this essay by Reverend Isaac Watts.*

The Reverend Samuel Lilly was rector from 1803 to 1805 and in charge of the academy at St. John's Episcopal Church. He was followed by Reverend John C. Rudd (1805–1826) who enlarged the church, improved the rectory, and conducted a classical school at his home. He also edited *The Christian Magazine* in the parsonage. He left because of poor health. Reverend Smith Pyne, rector from 1826 to 1828, served briefly in Elizabethtown. He later received his doctorate and became rector of St.John's Episcopal Church in Washington, D.C. The finances of the Elizabethtown church improved under the leadership of Reverend Birdseye Glover Noble, 1829 to 1833. When he resigned, he opened a boarding school. Reverend Samuel Adams Clark found the size of the church inadequate to meet the size of the congregation eager to hear him. He spearheaded the construction of a new church, the formation of Evergreen Cemetery in 1853, and the removal of some graves from the churchyard to Evergreen Cemetery in order to erect the present Gothic church.

Reverend John Giles became pastor of the Presbyterian Church, but left after only a few months. The next pastor in 1800 was Reverend Henry Kollock, son of Shepard Kollock, editor and publisher of the *New Jersey Journal* and grandson of Hannah White Arnet. Reverend Kollock served for three years until he was called to the Princeton Presbyterian Church and the College of New Jersey (later Princeton University). Reverend Kollock was followed by Reverend John McDowell, who served from 1804 to 1833. He married Henrietta Kollock, daughter of Shepard and sister of Henry. Under his guidance the congregation grew steadily. Unlike the other clergymen who had followed Reverend Caldwell, McDowell brought a great deal of stability to the church. His sermons attracted a larger congregation and soon the church trustees were discussing additions to the church or the construction of another church. The Female Society, the first women's-only organization in Elizabethtown, was organized in 1810 to perform good works. The women did so until 1910, when the society was disbanded. Reverend McDowell also organized a Sunday School with Reverend David Magie's Sunday School to teach African-American children and adults the Bible and how to read, write, and figure. The classes were conducted all afternoon on Sundays after the church services. They became so popular that Reverend McDowell started schools to accommodate first white girls and then white boys. He was opposed to profanity and horse racing. He wrote numerous essays and began publishing a bi-monthly magazine. He was zealous about completing the church building, erected the tall spire, and raised funds for the purchase of a bell. In 1833, he accepted a call to Central Presbyterian Church in Philadelphia.

Mayors of Elizabethtown Borough in the early nineteenth century included Elias Dayton, the merchant and general from 1796 to 1805; Caleb Halsted Jr., 1805 to 1822 and 1823 to 1830; Jeremiah Ballard, 1822 to 1823; and Isaac H. Williamson, a lawyer from 1830 to 1833. Williamson served as state governor from 1817 to 1829. He was also Elizabethtown's first librarian, serving for several years in the circulating library organized by Shepard Kollock from 1792 until about 1812.

The first six governors of New Jersey were veterans of the Revolution. In addition to William Livingston and Aaron Ogden, they were William Paterson, Richard Howell, Joseph Bloomfield, and William S. Pennington. After that most candidates for public office in New Jersey were veterans of the nation's other wars.

Elizabethtown, unlike its neighbor Newark, grew slowly. In the 1830 census there were 3,555 persons. By 1850 there were 5,583, and by 1860, 11,567. Elizabeth would experience its greatest growth at the end of the nineteenth century and the first decade of the twentieth century when immigrants from Southern and Eastern Europe arrived.

The state legislature authorized state banks in Elizabethtown, Newark, Trenton, New Brunswick, and Camden in 1812. These later became national banks. The Elizabeth Bank on Broad Street is on its original site. In 1982, it became Constellation, then Corestate, and after that First Union. In 2002, the name was changed to Wachovia. Its first president was Peter Kean, a grandnephew of Governor Livingston. Members of the Kean family were the bank's presidents until Emlen Roosevelt, a Kean cousin, retired and Constellation purchased it. Peter Kean was a trustee of the Elizabethtown Public School Association and president of the Elizabethtown Apprentices Library Association in 1821. He

This is the face of a clock made by John Brokaw of Elizabeth. The town was one of the leading areas for clockmakers and silversmiths before those crafts were replaced by mass production.

became president of the six-year-old Essex County Agricultural Society in 1823, and spoke to the group about rotation of crops and breeding of livestock. He had charge of the golden anniversary parade to celebrate the nation's 50th birthday in 1826. Unfortunately for Elizabethtown, Peter Kean died in 1828 at 40 years of age.

The War of 1812 lasted two years. Although preparations were made for the arrival of British forces in New Jersey, the war didn't touch this state. A fort was built on Sandy Hook overlooking the harbor. Thirty-two veterans of the war are buried in the graveyard adjacent to the Presbyterian Church. They include Colonel Jacob D. Edwards, Captain John Foster, Captain Isaac Crane, First Lieutenant Matthias Crane, Sergeant Captain William Pierson, and Corporal Benjamin Tucker. The other 26 apparently were privates. New Jersey sent 6,911 men to the war. Some of them assisted in the fortifications in New York Harbor.

Aaron Ogden of Elizabethtown, who opposed the second war with Great Britain, was elected governor of New Jersey from 1812 to 1813. Ogden was awarded an L.L.D. by the College of New Jersey in 1816. In addition to being an outstanding attorney, he operated a ferry line between Elizabethtown and New York City. Thomas Gibbons, a wealthy former mayor of Savannah, Georgia and the former governor of Georgia, became involved in a series of little disputes with Odgen. Gibbons's wife wanted a separation from Gibbons and selected Ogden to represent her. Gibbons decided to attack Ogden where it would hurt. He began operating a ferry between Halstead's Point and New York City, challenging Ogden's right to exclusive operation of a ferry. The courts agreed with him. Meanwhile Daniel Dod and Ogden completed the steamboat *Atlanta*. Construction was costly. Ogden sold the *Sea Horse* to help pay off the debt. He borrowed money from the Union Bank in New York City, but he was unable to meet the payments. He also was unable to pay his debt at the State Bank in Elizabethtown. Lawsuits continued. In 1822, the State Bank of Elizabethtown took over the operation of the Ogden ferries. Chief Justice John Marshall ruled that the states had no jurisdiction over interstate waters, the navigation of which was subject to control of federal authorities. Ogden was bankrupt. In 1824, he became president of the Society of Cincinnati of New Jersey and continued in that office until his death. He became vice-president of the national society in 1825 and its president in 1829. The bank foreclosed on his home, now the Belcher-Ogden mansion, in 1827. He moved to Jersey City, where he served in the customs office. He died on April 19, 1839, aged 83 years.

Although roads had been designated by this time, footpaths or sidewalks beside them were omitted until 1816, when an ordinance was adopted by the borough to "lay out, pave, gravel and keep repaired sidewalks and footpaths in the principal streets of Elizabethtown and to prevent obstructions in the same."

The possibility of a steam operated boiler for a ship began to interest mechanics during the Revolution. Clock and watchmaker Daniel Dod and Alfred Vail, working at Vail's estate Speedwell Village in Morristown, experimented with one. Dod moved to Elizabethport on the river where he opened the Steam Engine Factory to manufacture steam boilers. The *Savannah* became the first ship with a steam boiler made by Dod to cross the Atlantic Ocean in 1818. The trip was completed under sail because the ship ran out of coal to power the boiler.

Dod hired his nephew John Ward to sell the boilers. Aaron Ogden was a silent partner in the enterprise. Ward's father Silas opened another shop next door. Dod later moved to New York City, where he was killed when one of the boilers he was making exploded. John Ward spent 20 years in Canada, and when he returned he built the Croton Acqueduct for the New York City water supply. Silas Ward, who was one of the founders of both the Second and Third Presbyterian Churches, purchased the old Jewel's Mill at Salem Dam in Union Township and Lyon's Farms on the Elizabeth River. It was later purchased by the Elizabethtown Water Company.

In addition to the steam engine factory, several small factories were formed making stoveplates, sleighshoes, wheelboxes for wagons, carriages, plows, and flatirons. Along with Newark and Rahway, Elizabethtown was known for its carriage makers. The change from craftsmen to mass production was gradual. One of these was the Elizabethport Cordage Company, known locally as "The Rope Works," founded about 1829 and covering 20 acres along the Elizabeth River. The company made ropes from hemp for ships' rigging.

The First Presbyterian Church was overcrowded. Reverend McDowell decided that a new church should be formed to handle the overflow. He selected one of the First Presbyterian Church members, David Magie, to form the new congregation. Magie was studying to become a minister. The new session house of the First Presbyterian Church on Washington Avenue, now Dickinson Street, was provided as a meeting place until the new church could be erected. Land was selected for the church building on East Jersey Street and construction begun on the Second Presbyterian Church. The church, the oldest religious sanctuary still standing in Elizabeth, was dedicated on May 1, 1822. Some historians claim that the formation of the Second Presbyterian Church was caused by the religious revivals of 1817.

Reverend Dr. David Magie was a fortunate choice. He became one of the leaders of Elizabethtown. When the trustees of Second Church wanted to enlarge the sanctuary, he assisted in the organization of the Evergreen Cemetery in 1853, by clergymen and businessmen in Newark, Elizabethtown, and Union Township. Bodies from Second Church cemetery adjacent to the church were moved to the new cemetery. Reverend Magie's monument in the cemetery after he died was provided by the congregation of the church instead of by his family.

General Lafayette made his final visit to the United States in 1824–1825. As he passed a toll taker on a turnpike in Connecticut, the toll taker said, "You are the nation's guest" and refused to accept the toll. Word spread throughout the nation. Nobody charged Lafayette. He visited Elizabethtown twice. On the first visit, he walked through the graveyard at the Presbyterian Church with Jonathan Dayton visiting each grave of men who had served with him during the Revolutionary War. On his return visit the next year, Dayton was dead and Lafayette visited his grave.

At one time, banks were permitted to print and issue their own bank notes. This $100 bill was printed by the State Bank of Elizabeth after it formed in 1812.

Encouraged by the success of the Erie Canal in New York State, two canal companies were formed in New Jersey. The Morris Canal from Phillipsburg to Newark opened in 1831. Original plans would have taken the canal directly from Morristown to Elizabethtown, but political pressure caused it to be extended to Paterson and then cut down to Newark, leaving Elizabethtown out of the plan. It was built to Jersey City in 1836. The canal was an engineering marvel with its locks and planes but a financial failure. It rose from the Hudson River to 913 feet at Lake Hopatcong, a man-made lake, and down to 760 feet at Phillipsburg on the Delaware River. The barges carried coal to tidewater and manufactured products inland. It was impassible in winter when it froze, but it became a wonderful skating rink for children. The canal closed in 1924.

The men who had worked so hard to develop a steam engine for boats began thinking about the same device powering a coach on rails. The success of the Camden and Amboy Railroad across the middle of the state was followed immediately by two railroads through Elizabethtown: the Elizabethtown and Somerset Railroad and the New Jersey Railroad and Transportation Company. The Elizabethtown and Somerville Railroad (Central Railroad of New Jersey) was incorporated in 1831 and the New Jersey Railroad and Transportation Company (The Pennsylvania Railroad) in 1834. The first train ran from Elizabethtown to Plainfield on January 1, 1839. A horse and carriage ran alongside the tracks and won the unannounced race, but not for long. The railroad reached Phillipsburg by 1852, and the horses were unable to compete. The New Jersey Railroad tracks reached Philadelphia in 1840 from Jersey City. Ferries completed the trip to New York City. Both routes now are operated by the New Jersey Transit.

In order to avoid high prices for the railroad right of way, the companies built the railroads in short stages hoping to fool the land owners. Each stage was a different company such as the Somerville and Easton Railroad Company and the

The Second Presbyterian Church was organized by Reverend David Magie, a young student at the First Presbyterian Church in 1820. This building was dedicated in 1821 and is the oldest standing church in Elizabeth.

Elizabethtown-Somerville Railroad Company. The two lines merged in 1847. The company immediately extended the line from White House to Easton, Pennsylvania to carry coal from the Lehigh Valley to New York City. For reasons not explained, the new Elizabethtown-Somerville Railroad was pulled by a steam engine into the heart of Elizabethtown and detached. Horses pulled the train the rest of the way to the Arthur Kill. When the engines towed the freight cars to the train's yards, coal was removed from them and placed on barges at the railroad yard for the trip to New York City. The Central Railroad became involved in a race with the Delaware, Lackawanna and Western Railroad and later the Lehigh Valley Railroad as the carrier of coal from the mines in Pennsylvania to the new furnaces in New York and New Jersey.

From the start the railroads had a joint passenger station at Broad Street in the center of Elizabethtown, called Union Station. All traffic was stopped to permit the cars to pass. At first the people delighted in seeing them, but as time passed they began to protest the daily traffic jams and demanded an end to the delays.

Matthias William Baldwin (1795–1866), an Elizabeth native, moved to Philadelphia where he started M.W. Baldwin & Company and made his most famous locomotive, "Old Ironsides." The Baldwin company continued making locomotives for many years.

Lyon's Farms between Elizabethtown and Newark was cut in half in 1834 when a new township known as Clinton was formed. It was 3 miles wide and about 8 miles long and it began to disintegrate almost at once as new municipalities were formed from it. Finally in 1902, when only the Lyon's Farms section remained, it was annexed by the City of Newark.

A cattle drive along the Road to Newark toward the railroad station in Elizabethtown became a stampede when the bell made by David Ross on the roof of the North End Schoolhouse rang as they passed. The frightened animals ran into the center of Elizabethtown, and according to those who were present, took some time to round up and place on freight cars. The bell was taken to Trenton when the school was razed. Later it was returned to Elizabeth and, according to Elmer Hutchinson, was placed in the tower of the Westminster Presbyterian Church.

Reverend Nicholas Murray, pastor of the Presbyterian Church, followed Reverend McDowell in May 1833 and served until 1861. He died suddenly on February 4, 1861, a month after he left the pulpit. He became one of the church's most outstanding pastors through his writing. His writing was developed under the guidance of Reverend Dr. E.D. Griffith at Williams College. Reverend Dr. Griffith read Murray's early work containing long sentences and flowery rhetoric. When he finished reading a composition, he asked Murray sentence by sentence what he was attempting to say. Murray would state the thought simply. Dr. Griffith urged him to write that way. Reverend Murray wrote the first history of Elizabethtown, *Notes Concerning Elizabethtown*, published by Edward Sanderson in 1840. Reverend Murray's grandson, Nicholas Murray Butler, served as president of Columbia University from 1901 to 1945.

In 1835, Edward N. Kellogg purchased about 300 acres in Woodruff's Farms in the northern section of the city closest to today's Newark, and developed The New Manufacturing Town of Elizabethport with streets, lots, and parks. The area along the waterfront was called "The Crescent." It included Livingston Street, originally known as Washington Street, to New Point Road to Seventh Street to First Avenue and back to Elizabethpoint. Kellogg also subdivided plots from Magnolia Avenue (then Wall Street) and the city line of Newark into house lots 25 feet by 100 feet for dwellings for employees in the New Manufacturing Town of Elizabethport. He named the main streets for 14 U.S. presidents and the cross streets for his seven sisters and eight other female relatives. A large park area was preserved at the northern end and was known as North Park until the 1870s, when it was renamed Kellogg Park. Another park near Magnolia Avenue became Jefferson Park. P.B. Amory, a grandfather of Cleveland Amory, the animal activist and writer, and others also began purchasing farm acreage and subdividing the farms for dwellings and industries throughout the city.

The city purchased the old Adelphian Academy around 1845 for a public school. Five years later it was razed for a city hall. The first floor was used for markets and the second floor for city government until the first floor too was needed for city government. The courthouse burned during the Revolution, was rebuilt, burned again in 1808, and replaced on the same site.

Only three religious denominations were active in Elizabethtown until the 1840s, The First Presbyterian, St. John's, and the Methodist church. The Methodist church was organized on Water Street (Elizabeth Avenue) near the present Morrell Street by Reverend Thomas Morrell, a former Elizabethtown merchant who was wounded while serving as a captain during the Revolutionary War. He became a Methodist and a circuit rider for ten years. In 1804, he organized the church and was its pastor for 34 years.

Roman Catholics came to Elizabethtown with Governor Philip Carteret, but there was no nearby church until 1826, when St. John's Roman Catholic Church opened on Mulberry Street in Newark. Roman Catholics who wanted to attend Mass there had a long walk through the meadows from Elizabethtown. There were two Baptist churches before the Revolutionary War: the Scotch Plains Baptist Church, founded on September 8, 1747, by members of the Piscataway Baptist Church; and the Lyon's Farms Baptist Church, founded by the Scotch Plains church on April 16, 1769. The Broad Street Baptist Church was formed just before the Civil War and built an attractive building near the Stone Bridge. It closed in a few years when it was unable to pay its debts and the property was sold. There were Quaker meeting houses in Rahway and Plainfield, but none in the future Elizabeth. The Rahway Society of Friends also closed. The Plainfield Society continues to function.

The first Roman Catholic church was built on Washington Street, then called Old Broad Street, in 1845, and named St. Mary's. Reverend Isaac Howell became

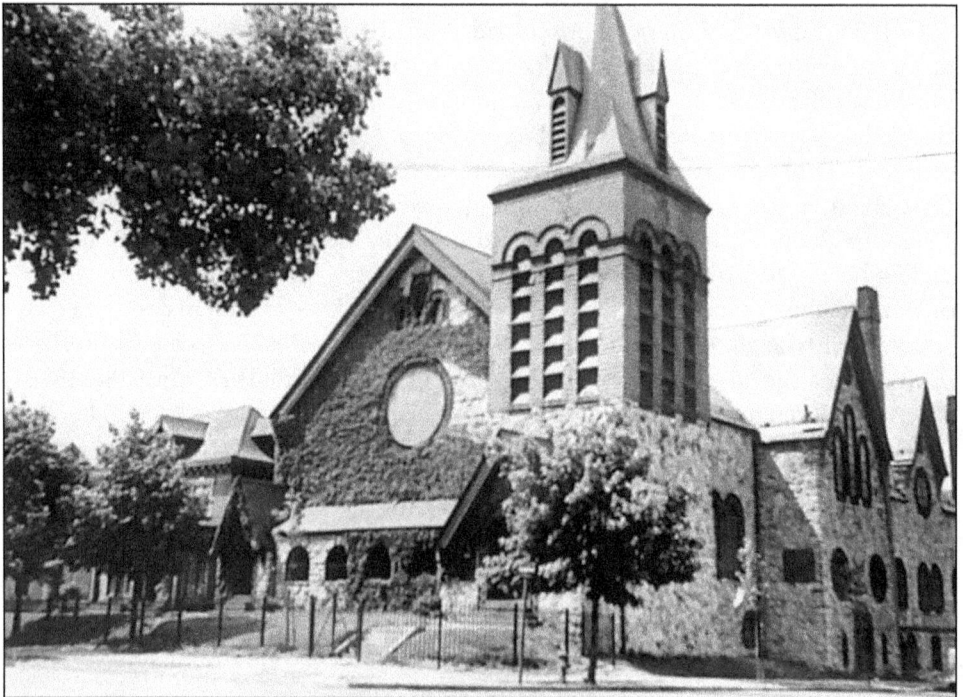

Greystone Presbyterian Church began as the First Congregation Church of Elizabethtown c. 1838. In 1842 it became the Marshall Street Presbyterian Church and by 1896 had moved to this building at Elizabeth Avenue and Florida Street. Fire destroyed the sanctuary in 1992.

the first pastor. Although most of the parishioners were Irish, the church had a French flavor for those who lived in Elizabethtown. A school was soon built near it and a cemetery started across the street from it. It also opened a high school, which continues to operate.

The Third Presbyterian Church was organized in 1851, just around the corner from Second. It was composed of members from the First and Second churches. Since 1991, the Elizabeth Playhouse has been located in the education building of the church. Another church formed in this period in the port was a Congregational church in 1836, which became the Marshall Street Presbyterian Church in 1846, when it was put under the Presbytery of Elizabethtown. The name was changed when a new greystone structure was erected on Elizabeth Avenue in 1896 and it became the Greystone Presbyterian Church. It was destroyed by fire in 1992. The congregation meets in the parsonage.

The First Baptist Church in Elizabethtown began in a building on Union Avenue in 1844. It is located today near that site on Union Avenue. Grace Episcopal Church congregation began meeting at the home of Vincent Bodine in 1845. Then a room in a public building was offered to the fledgling church. The parish was incorporated on August 18, 1849. Reverend Abraham Beach Carter was the founding rector. Reverend Edward B. Boggs assumed the post about a year later. He was replaced by Reverend David Clarkson in 1848, who had charge of the erection of a building at 221 East Jersey Street. Reverend Clarkson Dunn became rector in 1857 and served 13 years.

St. John's Episcopal Church became known along with the First Presbyterian Church as the "Mother of Churches." One of the first churches it organized was the Christ Episcopal Church in 1853. The simple Gothic church looked much like the churches in England's countryside. Its congregation met in the chapel of the First Presbyterian Church until its building was ready.

The Second Methodist Church on Fulton Street began in 1859, and St. Paul's Methodist Church on Mechanic Street (East Grand Street) was formed a short time later. St. Michael's Roman Catholic Church with its German speaking congregation began in 1855, and St. Patrick's Roman Catholic Church with its large Irish congregation in 1858. The German Evangelical Lutheran Church organized in 1856, and also conducted its services in the German language. There also was a German Methodist Episcopal Church in Elizabethport organized in 1853, at Third Avenue and Center Street, while the parsonage was on Amity Street.

It was during this period that Elizabethtown had its first and only Jewish mayor, David Naar, a Sephardic Jew whose ancestors were driven from Spain in 1492. He served as mayor of Elizabeth in 1842–1845. A native of the Caribbean, he was also the U.S. consul to St. Thomas Island from 1845 to 1848, when it was still owned by Denmark. He was a member of the Essex County Board of Freeholders in 1842, and a judge of the Court of Common Pleas of Essex County.

The potato famine that hit Ireland in the 1840s caused a huge migration of Irish to Elizabethtown. Jewish people, mainly from Bavaria, also came to

Elizabethtown with the Germans in the 1840s. At first they worked as peddlers with packs on their backs traveling along the dusty roads visiting housewives in an attempt to sell a variety of items. Later they established stores in the port area. Some, like Levy Brothers Department Store, moved up to Broad Street. Many were skilled craftsmen or artisans making cigars, shoes, or hats. Some were farmers. A few started small factories.

Mayer Southeimer of 119 Broad Street conducted a meeting of Jewish gentlemen at his home to form a congregation in 1857. He was an outstanding businessman who had been named to many committees by the Christians in the borough. Out of that meeting was formed the B'nai Israel Congregation, a conservative temple. He was also one of the directors of the Evergreen Cemetery, an interdenominational cemetery.

The Evergreen Cemetery was formed in 1853 by clergymen and businessmen in Elizabeth, Newark, and Union because the little church graveyards were full and both Second Presbyterian and St. John's Episcopal Churches wanted to use some of their church graveyard sites for additions. The graves in the way of the additions were moved and reburied in Evergreen Cemetery.

The cemetery was designed by Ernest L. Meyer (1828–1902), a native of Germany who came to the United States in 1851 and met Mr. Sayre, then surveyor for the municipality. When Sayre was unable to work, the young German-educated engineer was given the job of designing the former John Teas Farm on the Upper Road to Newark as Evergeen Cemetery. The board of trustees must have liked his work, because as more acres were purchased for the cemetery, Meyer was asked to design them too in the popular Victorian style of the day. The cemetery is composed of serpentine-patterned carriage paths, pedestrian paths, and rectangular and circular burial plots. Some of the original plots were surrounded by decorative black iron fences with gates. The roadways were named for trees such as Elm, Locust, Laurel, and Oak Avenues. Sheep originally were used to keep the lawn mowed. Then boys, usually Pingry School students, were employed to mow the grass during the summer. Heavy power mowers eventually replaced the sheep and the boys. The fences were removed in most instances to provide easier access to the individual plots. In all, Meyer planned 90 acres of the present 115-acre complex.

During this time Meyer became engineer for the city, planning all city improvements such as street and sidewalk alignment, the city storm and sanitary sewer systems, and the elevation of the Pennsylvania Railroad tracks with the city's famous arch over Broad Street. In his spare time, he became interested in land titles and traced many of them. He prepared a map of the city containing this information, which was published in 1879. The New Jersey Historical Society has reprinted the map.

Other mayors before the Civil War included Stephen P. Brittan, 1833–1838; Smith Scudder, 1838–1839; William Chetwood, 1839–1841, a lawyer who fought in the Whiskey Rebellion in 1794; Elias Winans, 1845–1846; Francis Barber Chetwood, 1846–1847 and 1851–1853, a lawyer; Edward Sanderson, 1847–1851, one time publisher of the *Elizabethtown Gazette* and the *New Jersey Journal* and later a job printer in 1844; and Elias Darby, 1853–1855 and 1855–1860, the last mayor of Elizabethtown Borough and the first mayor of Elizabeth City when it was formed in 1855. James Jenkins, 1861–1862, was the last peace-time mayor. Francis Barber Chetwood was mayor of the city in 1871–1872.

Several people of note came to Elizabethtown at this time. Among them was Lorenzo Da Ponte whom Charles Aquelina, former chairman of social studies in the Elizabeth schools, says was an Italian Jew. Da Ponte served as a librettist to Wolfgang Amadeus Mozart. He operated a grocery and dry goods store at Broad and East Jersey Streets for two to three years before he joined the faculty at Columbia College (Columbia University).

William Dunlap, a playwright and artist, gave a glowing picture of Elizabethtown praising the birds, the wild roses, and Catalpa trees. He attended a church service by Reverend Thomas Morrell on the devil and disliked it.

Until after the Civil War, the city had numerous small factories. They included an oil cloth factory; the Steam Cordage Company; the New Jersey Car-Wheel Manufacturing Company; malleable iron works; straw hat and bonnet factories; The Elizabethport Manufacturing Company, which made hardware for carriages; saw mills; shear works; rubber products; fertilizer; the Keen Pruden pottery works; the New Jersey Flax and Hemp Manufacturing Company; John Curtis bricks; Manhattan Stove Works; August Heidritter and Sons, lumber; and other

The Reverend David Magie was a doer. In addition to serving as pastor of the Second Presbyterian Church, he organized the Manual Labor School for boys, served with the Elizabethtown Public School Association, and was a founder of Evergreen Cemetery.

69

products. The Phineas Jones & Company moved to Elizabethport in 1855, to make wheels for circus wagons. It moved to Newark five years later and became the first company in the state to make wheels by machinery. In 1922, the firm went to Hillside but closed during the Depression. Circuses were moving in trucks, not wagons, and the company failed to start making automobile wheels. The peaceful green meadowland with grazing cows gave way to factory after factory and stacks emitting black smoke. The new city entered the industrial age.

It was in this period that Elizabethtown began to accept the concept of free public education. In the early nineteenth century, people with good incomes sent their sons or daughters to one of Elizabeth's many private schools or welcomed a tutor into their families to teach the children. Only the poor children attended the few public schools that existed. The old Academy closed in the mid-1830s because of competition from the Adelphian Academy, which continued operation until about 1855, when it became a public school until it was razed for a city hall.

Elias Darby Smith, a nephew of Mayor Elias Darby and the superintendent of schools from 1875 to 1877, selected 1850 as the date when Elizabethtown began conducting public schools in response to state laws and local opinion. The first state legislation was adopted in 1817, setting aside one-tenth of all money raised by taxes for the schools. Unfortunately, the law failed to provide for

Christ Episcopal Church was organized by St. John's Episcopal Church in 1853. St. Augustine Episcopal united with it in 1972 as the Church of the Resurrection.

administration of the fund. Another law in 1818 provided for the creation of a board of trustees. The following year a provision was made to invest the fund for an income.

Years passed. By 1829, taxes on banking, insurance, and other corporations were to be applied to the school fund and it was to be divided among the counties. The counties in turn were to divide the money among the communities. The communities were directed to raise additional funds. Several of the communities engaged in debates on whether the money should be used for the general benefit or only for poor children. Proponents of private schools favored the public schools as welfare for the poor. Yet another problem faced the advocates for public education for all, the lack of competent teachers.

Smith cited some statistics in 1840. There were 3,908 whites and 178 African Americans in Elizabethtown. The three unnamed private schools had 140 pupils. The first superintendent of schools was William Day, a lawyer, who served from 1847 to 1853. Initially there were six schools. These included one in the Port called the Industrial School District or School One. It was housed in the basement of the Marshall Street Presbyterian Church. There was an African-American School on Washington Street (Dickinson); School 5 in Wheat Sheaf on Rahway Road (Roselle), School 1, Adelphian Academy; School 3, the North End School; and schools on Crane and Harrison Streets in the Winans neighborhood, apparently in Linden.

The first public school in Elizabeth was School One on Third Street between Fulton and East Jersey Streets. A building was built in 1851 and altered in 1871 and 1879. It had grades one through twelve. The second public school was placed on Morrell Street in 1858 and altered in 1880. All other public schools were erected after the Civil War.

The Pingry School for Boys, a private school, was begun on the eve of the Civil War in the home of Jonathan Townley by Reverend Dr. John F. Pingry in 1861. Pingry School followed a school operated by Reverend John Gaylor Halsey from 1828 to about 1842, on Chilton Street. Reverend David H. Pierson, Ph.D., opened a school at the same site two years later and taught in it for 25 years.

Industries and additional residences increased the possibility of fire. Originally volunteer bucket brigades were formed when there was a fire. The buckets would be filled at the river, pond, or well and passed along a line of men to the fire and then passed back to be refilled. This was a slow process. As early as 1789, a volunteer fire company was stationed at South Broad Street near the Stone Bridge over the river. Each household was required to have two buckets in case of fire and ladders were placed around Elizabethtown for use during a fire if needed. This company operated about 20 years, after which it was dissolved.

In 1837, Protection Company Number One was reorganized and was the forerunner of Fire Engine Company One. Its first piece of equipment was a hand drawn pumper to spray water on the fire. The same year the Lafayette Hook and Ladder Company One was established. The next year it gave its pumper to Cataract Engine Company Two on East Grand Street, while Protection Company purchased a new Smith hand drawn pumper. Cataract Company, after a dispute with the City Council, became Rolla Engine Company Two. It relocated on West Grand Street until the site was needed for the Pennsylvania Station. The fire company moved back to East Grand Street. It purchased a Smith Hand-Drawn Steamer, the first steam engine used in the city. Its slogan was "Rolla to the Rescue." It became the first company to wear uniforms.

Two more companies were organized before the Civil War. These were Washington Engine Company Three in 1841 at 8 Center Street and Red Jacket Engine Company Four in 1855. Its location is not listed. The area was divided into districts and a bell in each district was designated to alert both the volunteer firemen and the horses. The bells were rung four times. They were in St. John's Episcopal Church tower, another was a tower near Union Square, and the third was on the roof of the Red Jacket Engine Company Four. The site of the fourth is unlisted.

There were few fires. When the bells sounded the volunteers ran to the firehouse to get the pumper and pull it to the fire by hand. The fires usually were wood or grass. Efforts made to form fire insurance companies in some towns were futile. The insurance company would place a plaque on the insured house. Representatives of the insurance company responded when there was a fire. Unfortunately fires seldom were confined to one building and would instead spread along a street burning insured and uninsured houses alike. Mutual aid by the volunteer companies was unknown. If a company responded to a fire in a neighboring town by mistake, the men would sit down and watch instead of attempting to assist in extinguishing the fire.

There was little need for law enforcement in old Elizabethtown. The crown appointed constables to uphold the laws. Mayor Caleb Halsted Jr. organized a watch to guard the borough in 1811. These men carried a rattle to summon help if needed. Mayor David Naar formed a police department in 1845, of a marshall and constables who worked days, and a night watch of two or three men in each ward to enforce the law at night. The present police department was organized in 1858. Walter S. Miller was appointed chief and Jabez B. Cooley, assistant chief. Ten special policemen each were appointed for the three wards. They usually worked on Saturday and Sunday nights and on holidays. When the number of wards increased to six in 1861, six additional men were appointed.

There were no hospitals at this time. The sick were cared for at home. The well-to-do had servants or relatives to help. An unmarried woman, for instance, might live with her brother's or sister's family and assist with child care and housework. There were few jobs for women. Some women inherited their husbands' businesses after they died and continued to operate them. Some assisted in the stores along Broad Street or Elizabeth Avenue. Others took in boarders and some served the noonday meal to factory workers. A few became teachers in the new schools.

The Elizabethtown Water Company was formed in 1854 to provide water for both the people and the new industries that required an abundant supply. Dams

St. Mary's Roman Catholic Church, founded in 1844, was the first Catholic church in Elizabethtown. The sanctuary and school were built on Washington Avenue in 1862 and reconstructed in the 1950s.

were built on the Elizabeth River at Trotter's Lane for a reservoir known as Ursino Lake, at Parker Road, Crane's Pond at West Grand Street, Dravis Pond at Westfield Avenue, and at Chilton Street. The founders included Francis B. Chetwood, George R. Chetwood, Francis Harris Jr., John D. Norris, Reuben Van Pelt, Keen Purden, Colonel John Kean, and others.

The Elizabethtown Gas Light Company was begun in 1855 to provide light, heat, and power to operate machinery. Colonel John Kean (1814–1895), son of Peter and a member of the militia, was its president.

In the 1850s, officials in Elizabethtown wanted their freedom from Newark and Essex County. Elizabethtown Borough, formed in 1789, wanted to become a city and be in a separate county. In 1855, it achieved the first wish when it united with Elizabethtown Township. The township covered most of the port area, but did not appear to have an active government during its 61 years of existence. Two years later the County of Union was formed on May 18, 1857, from the southern part of Essex County. The election of 1807, placing the courthouse in Newark, still bothered Elizabethans, who wanted their freedom from that city. Having to go to Newark to attend to business and serve on juries was an annoyance. Elizabethtown lost out to Newark in the turnpike, railroad, highways, and ferry service. Historians believe that the name Union came from the discussion of the nation's unity, but the origin of Union for the township is unknown. The new county, the youngest in New Jersey and the second smallest county in the state, contained seven communities. Besides the City of Elizabeth that became the county seat, there were New Providence, Rahway, Springfield, Union, Westfield, and Plainfield.

The Elizabeth Orphan Asylum Association was incorporated on February 12, 1858. It acquired a house on Broad Street for 11 children from the alms house. A lot was purchased and a large building erected on Murray and Cherry Streets. The third and last building was the Janet Memorial Home on Salem Avenue, built in 1930 and used until 1962, when the state eliminated orphan asylums.

By 1860, there were still many descendants of the original Associates in Elizabeth. These were augmented by immigrants from Ireland, Scotland, England, Wales, France, Germany, Africa, and northern Ireland. The new city had a small Jewish population and three Roman Catholic churches: St. Mary's, 1844; St. Michael's, 1855; and St. Patrick's, 1858. Several of the churches were German speaking. Among them was the German Moravian Church, 1861.

More and more industries were being built in Elizabeth. At first the owners of the new factories lived on the property adjacent to the factories. As they became more affluent, they began to move uptown along Elizabeth Avenue, Jefferson Park, into the future Elmora, Westminster, and other areas. The factories stayed in

Winfield Scott had an outstanding military record in the War of 1812 and the Mexican War. When he proved unable to successfully lead Union forces during the first six months of the Civil War he was transferred to West Point, where he died in 1866.

the meadowland. By 1861, the factory whistle had replaced the church and school bells in Elizabeth.

With the frontier and war days behind them and with improved roads and transportation, the people began to form social groups. There were choral groups starting in the churches. In addition to those there was the Elizabethtown Chapter of the African Colonization Society to help send African Americans back to Africa, The Elizabethtown Temperance Union, a library association, literary societies, an agricultural society, the Masons, Odd Fellows, and others. Most were short lived. Others were replaced by other organizations after the Civil War.

New Jersey was a border state during the Civil War. The state was divided in half by the unofficial extension of the Mason-Dixon line through New Jersey.

Many Elizabeth businessmen opposed the approaching hostilities because they sold carriages, saddles, shoes, and clothing to the Southern states and they objected to losing their markets. In addition to that, about a half of the students at the College of New Jersey came from the Southern states and Cape May was a favorite summer vacation spot for Southerners. New Jersey was also a Democratic Party state, as were the 11 states that formed the Confederacy. The Southern Democrats were pro-slavery. They became known as "Copperheads." Some of the New Jerseyans who believed in state's rights felt that the slavery problem was something for the South to solve. David Naar, by that time editor and publisher of *The True American* in Trenton, opposed the war.

New Jersey opposed the election of Abraham Lincoln in 1860. But when President-elect Lincoln went through the city enroute to Washington, D.C. to become president, crowds of people attempted to see him and cheer him. When the draft became effective in 1863, New Jerseyans said they could fill the desired quota without the draft and did. South Jersey had segregated schools until the late 1930s, while schools in the northern parts of the state were integrated.

4. PRESERVATION OF THE UNION 1858–1865

The nation was divided in the 1850s by the issue of slavery. The original Mason-Dixon line had nothing to do with slavery, but as new states were formed, the line was selected as the border between slave states and free states. It was eventually extended to Missouri. African Americans living north of the line were free, while those living south of it were enslaved. The line was never meant to extend into New Jersey, but it did. While the state outlawed dealing in slaves, those who escaped from the South were to be returned to their masters until the Civil War.

Before Fort Sumter in Charleston, South Carolina was attacked by Confederates on April 12, 1861, most Elizabeth residents thought the difficulties between Northern and Southern states would be ironed out. They even met at Library Hall on January 31, 1861, to adopt a resolution to preserve the Union, but not by force of war. After the attack, New Jersey governor Charles S. Olden issued a call for troops.

War fever seemed to sweep the city as men volunteered. Companies were formed and sent to Camp Olden in Trenton for shipment to Washington, D.C. The new Union County sent ten companies assigned to seven regiments to fight in the war. These were Company A of the 1st Regiment, said to be the first mustered in the nation; Company A of the 2nd Regiment; Company K of the 3rd Regiment, Companies G and K of the 9th Regiment, Companies B and D of the 11th Regiment; Companies C and E of the 14th Regiment; and Company B of the 13th Regiment. The communities paid bonuses to those who enlisted. Some men went to Newark where the bonus was higher. In addition, some men volunteered for New York State units and a few joined in Philadelphia.

In the meantime, Reverend James Roosevelt Bayley, nephew of Mother Seton and bishop of the new see in Newark, wrote to the Propagation of Faith in Rome, "We are sadly in need of priests. Had we a sufficient number of zealous and worthy priests, religion would make great headway in this country. At present it is almost impossible to take care of the Catholics."

St. Mary's Roman Catholic Church, organized in 1844, conducted its services in English. The congregation at St. Michael's was German and did not understand

English. Land was purchased on Smith Street and a small church built. Three priests were assigned to the little church until Reverend Peter Henry Lemke (1796–1882), a native of Germany, was installed as pastor. He started the school at St. Michael's in 1864 and asked for Benedictine Sisters from Newark to teach. Mother Warburga Hock and two other nuns arrived at St. Michael's to teach.

Captain Seth Boyden Ryder, the only man to serve as sheriff of Union County (1872–1875 and 1878–1881) and mayor of Elizabeth (1882–1883), joined the army in New York City. He suffered wounds in the Shenandoah Valley in the Battle of Russell's Ford, where Confederate soldiers captured him and held him prisoner for 18 months in the Libby Prison in Richmond, Virginia. After the war he became the owner of Ryder & Stead, a painting and paperhanger company. The war-time mayors in Elizabeth were James R. Burnet, 1861–1862, and Philip H. Grier, 1862–1871.

Because it was believed that the war would be short, the initial enlistments were for three months only. Meetings were conducted to recruit men at Library and Washington Halls. By week's end 56 men had registered. One of these was David Hatfield, a watchman at the Elizabeth oilcloth factory, who was elected captain of the volunteers in Company A, 1st Regiment of Union County. Thomas Tillou and Luther Martin were named first and second lieutenants respectively of the same company. Major Hatfield suffered a head wound on June 27, 1862 at Gaines' Mills during the advance on Richmond, Virginia. He was sent home by train where he died six weeks later. Martin was the only Elizabethan killed at Gettysburg on July 2, 1863. Both soldiers were buried in the new Evergreen Cemetery by their families.

The state lacked funds to purchase uniforms and equipment for an army. Loans had to be sought from local banks for both. Initially there was no uniform code. The uniforms for the various companies varied greatly. The men marched to the Union Station off Broad Street and boarded trains for Trenton with little or no training. After a brief stay in Trenton while the regiments were formed, they were sent on to Washington, D.C.

Patriotism swept through the area. Daily flag ceremonies were featured at public buildings. Men drilled on the green in front of the First Presbyterian Church. Nearly every farm displayed the flag. The clergymen who opposed slavery preached against it every Sunday. The spiritual life of the soldiers was remembered by the donations of a Bible to each volunteer.

Some firms like the oilcloth factory paid the volunteer's salary for six months. Relief committees were formed to pay the families $5 a week. The State of New Jersey later agreed to pay $72 a year or $216 for the term of enlistment, while the U.S. Government approved payment of $13 a month to dependents or widows of servicemen. The eight-year-old Evergreen Cemetery board of trustees set aside an area of the cemetery for free lots for veterans. None of the men buried in the section was killed in battle.

Women began to prepare clothing and food for the fighting units and gifts for the sick. Included among their gifts were little bags containing buttons, thread, and needles, as well as flannel shirts and handkerchiefs. The women also knitted socks and sweaters for the soldiers.

The economics of the city changed. J.A. Banniser of Elizabeth was awarded a contract for 100,000 pairs of shoes. Others made saddles, harnesses, hats, and wagons for the soldiers. There was a demand for fruit from the orchards and for horses.

General Winfield Scott of Elizabeth, a hero of the Mexican War, was placed in charge of the Union Army for the first six months. Unfortunately he was ineffective in the first battles. One part of his problem was the brief three-month enlistments and the untrained troops. General Scott was reassigned to the U.S. Military Academy at West Point, New York.

The first troops assigned to the battlefield were sent by canal boats from the Delaware-Raritan Canal to Annapolis, Maryland, because Confederate troops held Baltimore, its railroad station, and its railroad tracks there. (Maryland along with Delaware, Kentucky, and Missouri stayed with the Union, while the other Southern states seceded.) New Jersey troops were deployed along the telegraph and railroad tracks between Washington, D.C. and Annapolis to protect the communication lines. This protection of railroad rights of way and telegraph lines was done throughout the war.

The Civil War was the first war the United States fought that used railroads, telegraph lines, and photographs extensively. Historians call it the first modern war. In addition to the well-known Matthew Brady, many photographers drove their wagons to the battlefields to capture the war on glass plates. A few of them even used balloons to photograph the first aerial views of battlefields. Their wagons hauled the heavy cameras and served as darkrooms. Their photographs appeared in the newspapers and magazines of the day, bringing the agony of war home to the people.

Oddly enough though, writers continued to describe war as glorious and glamorous. It wasn't until Stephen Crane, born in Newark in 1870, wrote *The Red Badge of Courage*, describing the horrors of war, that people began to realize that war was hell. Crane's ancestors included the early settler Stephen Crane, one of the Associates; Mayor Stephen Crane, who was Elizabethtown mayor during the Revolution; and Richard Townley, who donated the land for St. John's Episcopal Church.

Most of the Elizabeth troops were sent to the District of Columbia, where they camped on Meridian Hill, which they renamed "Camp Monmouth." When it became evident that the Confederate Army was massing at Manassas Junction, Virginia, about 30 miles away in an effort to capture Washington, the New Jersey regiments were moved across the Potomac River to Arlington Heights, Virginia. They called their entrenchments Fort Runyon, named for Brigadier General Theodore Runyon of Newark, their commander.

The New Jersey regiments faced the Confederates for the first time at the first battle of Bull Run on July 21, 1861. People in Washington rode out to the battlefield in their carriages as though they were watching a bull fight in a ring. They all anticipated a rapid victory over the Confederate troops. Suddenly, as they were enjoying the spectacle, the Union line broke at Centreville. The Union

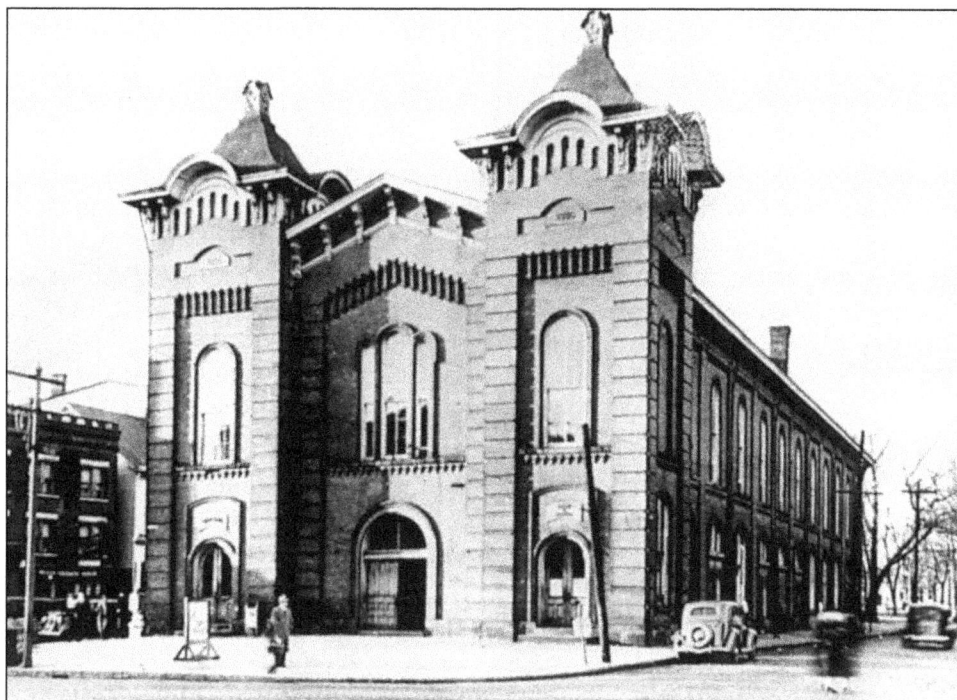

This building on Elizabeth Avenue between East and West Scott Places served as Elizabeth City Hall from 1865 to 1940.

forces representing parts of the 13 regiments composed of more than 10,000 men, retreated in panic. Left behind in the stampede were their supplies and wounded. Their disorderly retreat was hampered by the onlookers, some of whom were trampled in the rush.

The 1st Regiment reformed and attempted to make a stand the next day, but realizing that it was alone, it also retreated, picking up provisions as it went. Many Union soldiers were taken prisoner for the first time in this battle. Two days later, the three-month enlistments for many of the men expired and they returned home, happy to escape with their lives. Others reenlisted several times, so it is difficult to determine how many men actually served.

During the rest of 1861, there were many skirmishes with the enemy as well as reconnaissance missions. Private James Donnelly of Elizabeth was captured October 10, 1861 at Manassas Junction after losing his left eye in one of the skirmishes. He managed to escape on January 28, 1862, and returned to the Union lines. After a furlough at home he reenlisted.

The 9th Regiment had more Springfield rifles and ambulances than any other regiment when it left the state for the battlefield on December 6, 1861. It stayed in the District of Columbia for a month before being assigned to General Ambrose E. Burnside to make the Northern blockade of the Southern ports effective.

The regiment sailed south from Fortress Monroe, Maryland on January 12, 1862, and anchored at Hatteras Inlet off the North Carolina coast the next day. A violent gale struck the vessels on January 14, and several were blown ashore, while others became lodged on sandbars, and some were sunk.

Samuel J. Dilkes of Company K swam ashore in the gale to fasten a rope so the *Pocahontas*, loaded with horses, would be secure. He later assisted a woman cook from the ship to the shore. The brigantine *Dragon*, with most of the Union County troops, got stuck on a sand bar and was towed off by the *Patuxent* on January 16. The contingent made a successful landing February 7 and 8, 1862, at Roanoke Island and took possession of it on February 10.

The Union soldiers followed the retreating enemy to New Bern, North Carolina and captured the city on March 14, giving the Union forces a base south of Richmond, Virginia, the Southern stronghold. As the second year of the war began, the Confederate forces continued to threaten the capital and the Union forces had one post in the South at New Bern.

Captain Peter Ritter of Company K returned to his Elizabeth home for 60 days in April because of ill health. Private Thomas Macquaid of Elizabeth was struck in the shoulder by a spent ball at New Bern, but refused to stop fighting until the victory was assured. The body of Theodore M. Denman of Elizabeth, who died of fever at New Bern, was shipped to Elizabeth for burial, bringing the war close to home.

Sergeant J. Madison Drake of Elizabeth observed in a note to *The Jersey Journal* on May 1, 1862, that the 9th Regiment, New Jersey Volunteers, on guard duty in the New Bern area was having difficulty obtaining replacements for casualties. He added that it was decided to disband two of the 12 companies in the regiment and divide the men among the other ten companies. This action was taken on November 10, 1862, when the Secretary of War directed the consolidation and 171 members of Companies A and L, all German speaking, were reassigned.

Sergeant Drake found guard duty rather pleasant. "We have a lively time of it, plenty to eat, such as hot cakes, eggs, potatoes and milk. The boys are in fine spirits. We ramble along the shore of Bogue Sound picking blackberries, gathering oysters and clams and shooting ducks or geese." A lieutenant and three men even attempted to shoot a large alligator. The farmers were friendly and sold the soldiers produce. Their wives and daughters came to the camp to witness the regimental reviews and a member of Company E married a Miss Bell. But Drake conceded that "it was not as comfortable an existence as might be hoped. Mosquitoes, gnats, wood ticks and moccasin snakes are plentiful."

The popular Captain William B.S. Boudinot of Company K of Elizabeth was reported lost on a trip of exploration in a small boat on the sound. He returned to camp several days later reporting that he was fired upon by mistake by Union soldiers. He abandoned his boat to swim to safety on a island. Later he hiked several miles to return to camp.

General Winfield Scott of Elizabeth was retired by President Abraham Lincoln on November 1, 1861, and General George McClellan, another New Jerseyan, was selected to replace him. Unfortunately McClellan failed to follow through when he almost won a battle. Both generals were plagued by the brief three-month enlistments. On August 1, 1861, the length of enlistments was extended from three months to two years.

McClellan, commander of the Army of the Potomac, which was composed mostly of New Jersey regiments, decided to advance on Richmond, Virginia, from the James River instead of Washington. The siege of Yorktown began April 5 and continued until May 4. McClellan's forces captured Williamsburg on May 5 and fought at the Battles of Seven Pines and Fair Oakes on May 31 and June 1, respectively.

General "Fighting Joe" Hooker is said to have ordered the Jersey men back several times during these battles, but they would not leave the field. An unknown correspondent wrote, "Our volunteers will never disgrace the horses' heads and plows of our state insignia." Many of the conversations of the men began with the phrase, "When I get to Richmond," he reported. Historians then and now believe that McClellan had Richmond within his grasp, but instead waited for reinforcements and the opportunity was lost.

The Union forces continued to push forward to Mechanicsville on Beaver Dam Creek, where they were repulsed June 16 by forces under the command of General Robert E. Lee, who had taken command of the Confederate Army. The battle and the retreat was through swamps and woods and is called the "Seven

J. Augustus Dix became superintendent of Elizabeth schools in the late 1870s. One of his innovations was the creation of a two-year normal school to train teachers.

81

Days Battle." Colonel I.M. Tucker told his men, "It is rather hot in there and some of us will never come out, but the Jersey boys will do their duty." He died leading his troops. A corporal carrying the American flag buried it rather than have it captured. Lieutenant John B. Lutz of Company K, 3rd Regiment was listed as wounded and taken prisoner.

Union forces continued to retreat across White Oak Swamp to Savage Station, the terminus of the York and Richmond Railroad where the army's ammunition was stored, then to Malvern Hill and finally to Harrison's Landing on the Berkeley Plantation. A commentator at the time remarked, "so many fell. It should have shown grander results." The attack on Richmond was over. Historians say it should have been a Union victory ending the war, but McClellan waited again for reinforcements that didn't arrive. In the meantime, President Lincoln continued to look for a leader to command the Eastern army.

Lieutenant John B. Lutz was released from his prison camp and returned home to Elizabeth to recruit more men with Captain William R. Meeker, also of Elizabeth. There was much excitement when at a meeting at Library Hall, Lieutenant Lutz limped to the front of the room to urge the men to enlist. He was given a sword by a veterans' group. When peace came he was made overseer of the poor by the city. He also apparently operated a tailor shop on Morris Avenue.

Brevet General J. Madison Drake was one of four Medal of Honor recipients from Elizabeth during the Civil War. When he returned home he organized the Veteran Zouaves and published the Sunday Leader, *the* Elizabeth Daily Leader, *and the* Daily Monitor.

General Ambrose E. Burnside replaced General McClellan on November 7, 1862. Burnside commanded the Union forces at the Battle of Kinston, Virginia on December 14, and the Battle of Fredericksburg, Virginia on December 15. A correspondent called "The Observer" wrote in *The Jersey Journal* January 5, 1863, that the 11th Regiment, New Jersey Volunteers, left camp near Falmouth, Virginia on December 12, in the second march on Richmond:

> We remained in sight of the Battle of Fredericksburg for six hours on the first day watching the batteries of the two armies fire at each other. We continued to observe the battle as line after line of Union forces marched up to the rebel regiments, fought and fell back.
>
> On Sunday morning we were ordered across the Rappahannock River into battle for the first time. We kept up the incessant fire for two hours. Each man fired from sixty to one hundred twenty rounds, before we were pulled out and other men sent in.

During the Battle of Fredericksburg, Virginia, on December 13, 1862, the men of Companies A and D in the 11th Regiment, New Jersey Volunteers, and the rebels agreed to a cease fire. During the recess they talked and exchanged coffee, tobacco, jackknives, and regimental buttons.

The army camps were reportedly full of diseases such as measles, yellow fever, and typhoid fever. Long trains passed through Elizabeth with patients for the Marcus Ward Hospital in Newark. Disease was rampant at home, too. Death, disease, and desertion plagued the Union forces. Provost guards patrolled the city streets in search of deserters. "Anyone wearing military dress is liable for questioning," wrote Ben Bolt, a correspondent of the time.

During the Civil War, temporary hospitals were established for the soldiers. In many instances each regiment had its own hospital. Sometimes it was a house, other times schools, barns, and warehouses were used. The Marcus L. Ward Hospital in Newark was established by Ward, "the soldiers' friend."

Fanny Ricketts, an Elizabeth native, set up several makeshift hospitals during the Civil War in order to care for her husband and distant cousin, General James Ricketts, a career army officer. He was wounded three times. She followed him to battle in her carriage and when he was wounded took him to a nearby house to nurse him. She also treated other Union soldiers who were wounded. In one instance, she is said to have carried fresh water half a mile.

One of the many hardships facing the servicemen and their families was the failure to receive pay regularly. Some of the regiments were not paid for periods as long as six months. A Colonel Cook was sent to the battlefield as a representative of the State of New Jersey to collect portions of the servicemen's pay to be given to the families of the men. It was reported that some of the men gave him $10 of the $13 they were paid. When Cook returned to New Jersey in February 1863, he had more than $166,000 to distribute to the families of the soldiers.

Because of the failure to recruit as many men as needed for the armed services, a national draft was adopted on March 3, 1863. All men between the ages of 20 and 45 were required to register, provide a substitute, or pay $300. When word of the draft was received in New York City, there was a riot. In Newark a mob gathered. It was dispersed without any damage. The State of New Jersey asked President Lincoln for permission to enlist its quota of men instead of drafting them. It enlisted 4,998 men, doing better than states that implemented the draft.

After the war turned in the North's favor following Union victories at Gettysburg and Vicksburg, General U.S. Grant, now in charge of Union armies in the east, battled Confederate general Robert E. Lee in an attempt to capture Richmond.

Elizabethan J. Madison Drake, who enjoyed the lazy days at New Bern, was among the troops sent into Virginia in this effort. He was taken prisoner during the terrible conflict at Drewry's Bluff just south of Richmond. He was moved from prison to prison in six cities before he and three other officers found a portion of a map of South Carolina and decided they would attempt to escape. The opportunity came when they were being moved to a prison in Charleston, South Carolina "on dilapidated cars attached to a rickety wheezing wood-burning locomotive."

The future brevet brigadier general secretly removed the percussion caps from the muskets of seven Confederate soldiers guarding them in a box car. When the signal was given, he and his three companions leaped from the moving train and ran into a cypress swamp. Luckily, a severe storm came up. "The trees set up a mournful howling while the winds shrieked as if under the influence of a demon," he wrote in his book *Historical Sketches of the Revolutionary and Civil Wars*. "The storm was nothing compared to the dread we had for the fierce dogs now on our trail and the soldiers, whose excited voices we could hear on the edge of the swamp—men who were seeking our recapture."

The fugitives put onions in their shoes and traveled frequently through streams in an effort to put the dogs off their trail. They were nearly caught several times. On one occasion, a Confederate officer gave them a large plug of tobacco and directed them to "a good crossing of a river." They met more than 100 deserters from the Southern army and urged them to flee to the Union lines, he wrote.

Finally after traveling for 49 days and covering more than 1,000 miles, they reached safety at Knoxville, Tennessee. Drake, then 24 years old, weighed only 90 pounds. His boots were gone. His trousers were torn up to the knees and "his skin clung to the bones like wet parchment." During the long flight the men ate corn they found in the fields or were fed by Northern sympathizers and slaves. "There was something royal in the cheerfully rendered services of these poor creatures," the future publisher wrote of the slaves. "They seemed to look upon us in some way as sufferers for their sakes."

When he returned home Drake organized the Veteran Zouaves, which became one of the most famous drill teams in the nation. He was promoted to the rank of brevet general and was awarded the Congressional Medal of Honor. He became publisher of the *Sunday Leader* until February 1890; the *Elizabeth Daily Leader*, which began July 29, 1889; and *The Daily Monitor* for about ten years.

Captain William Brant of Elizabeth, a volunteer fireman before the war, was a member of Company B, 1st New Jersey Regiment, when it charged the Confederate trenches at Petersburg. He captured the battle flag of the 46th North Carolina Regiment and the flag of Confederate General A.P. Hill. He also was awarded the Congressional Medal of Honor. The New Jersey Regiment participated in 22 battles and witnessed Lee's surrender at Appomattox Court House on April 9, 1865, which ended the war. Brant was appointed captain in the police department in 1888, and with Police Chief Harry C. Austin, also a Civil War veteran, introduced features of the military into policing with rigid discipline and line of command.

Major Rufus King, a career army man who married Maria Williamson, daughter of Benjamin Williamson, second chancellor of New Jersey, also was presented the medal. Major King, then an artillery lieutenant, was in the Peninsula campaign on June 29, 1862. The captain of his unit was wounded during the retreat across the Chickahominy River in Virginia. King took command, rallying the frightened troops and faced the oncoming Confederate soldiers. The battery repelled the attack and covered the retreat of the remainder of the Union forces across the White Oak Swamp until they were forced to fall back. King continued to serve in the army until 1891, when he was honorably discharged with the rank of major. He returned to Elizabeth to a home on North Avenue, now in Hillside. Pingry School was built on what used to be his land in 1953. It became the East Campus of Kean University in 1978, and the center for the Gateway Institute after Pingry moved to Somerset County.

Reverend John Pingry, a Presbyterian minister, founded his namesake boys' school in 1861 and served as its first headmaster. Located in Elizabeth from 1861 to 1953, it moved from Hillside to a 193-acre campus in Bernards Township in the 1980s.

Boatswain's Mate John Williams II was captain of an 11-inch gun aboard the U.S.S. *Mohican* during the action of the main squadron of ships against the heavily defended Forts Beauregard and Walker on Hilton Head Island in South Carolina, and against ships of the Confederate fleet on November 7, 1861. Williams maintained steady fire against the enemy while under the fort batteries during a four-hour engagement, which resulted in silencing the batteries of the forts and the rout of the rebel steamers. He also was awarded the medal.

Meanwhile in Elizabeth, the tracks of the Central Railroad ended at Elizabethport. Ferries continued to carry passengers and cargo to New York City as they had for nearly 200 years. The ferries were slow and subject to tides and storms. John Taylor Johnson, president of the Central Railroad of New Jersey, realized that the railroad would be unable to compete successfully with other railroads if it continued to use the slow ferries. He led the railroad's efforts to gain permission to build a bridge across Newark Bay so that the Central Railroad too could be extended to tidewater at Jersey City.

The effort took more than five years. Johnson reached an agreement with the Camden and Amboy Railroad, New Jersey's first railroad, to split the returns on its western service on a 50-50 basis. The New Jersey Legislature granted approval for the bridge in 1860, on the eve of the Civil War.

The construction of the double track, 2-mile long bridge with two draws began under the direction of John Owen Sterns, the first superintendent of the railroad, who lived in Elizabeth. He died in November 1862, before the bridge was completed, and he was buried in Evergreen Cemetery. The Central Railroad provided a large monolith for him. It is one of the few monuments in the cemetery provided by friends instead of the individual's family.

First pulled by men in 1842, the "Old Amity" hose carriage is shown here in a 1952 parade.

The new bay bridge went from Crane's Point just northeast of the future Singer's Company plant across Newark Bay to Bayonne. The wood timber bridge draw openings were each only 75 feet wide. From Bayonne the railroad was extended to Communipaw on the Jersey City waterfront. Initially the tracks went up and down each hill. Later the hills were cut through so the tracks were level.

The railroad purchased the ferry service begun by William Jansen to Battery Place, New York City. A ferry dockage area was built in 1865, in the vicinity of Liberty Street in New York City. It also built a large terminal at Jersey City. The new bridge was dedicated on August 1, 1864, and passenger service began the next day. Regular freight service was delayed until 1866. One of the railroad's ferries, *The Kill Van Kull*, was taken by the U.S. Government to transport troops from New York City to Virginia during the war.

Several auxiliary buildings were also erected in Union County including stations at Elizabeth and Cranford, ice houses and freight houses at Roselle, water tanks and a tank house in Cranford, and an engine house and roundhouse in Elizabeth.

Almost as soon as the $319,500 bridge was open, complaints were made by ship owners against it. They said that the two draws were too small and out of alignment with the currents in the bay. The Central Railroad attempted to alleviate these problems by hiring a tugboat to assist the ships through the draws. Despite this effort there were several collisions with the bridge.

Before the long-awaited bridge was completed, the CRR made agreements with the New Jersey Railroad, later the Pennsylvania Railroad, to use its tracks to Jersey City. The switch was made at ground level in the center of Elizabeth.

Ferry service from Elizabethport to New York City was operated for many years by the Elizabethtownport-New York Ferry Company. Organized in 1818, and incorporated in 1839, it was operated until 1889, when the lack of passengers caused it to cease.

A Central Railroad historian noted that while most of the other railroads in New Jersey were built to carry coal across the state from Pennsylvania to tidewater, the Central Railroad was built from the Hudson River westward. It provided a vital link with the West and played an important part in the settlement of the West, especially in the years following the Civil War.

The railroad carried people from New York and Jersey City into the farmlands to settle in the country and created lovely suburbs such as the Roselles, Cranford, Garwood, Westfield, Fanwood-Scotch Plains, and Plainfield, and commuters into New York to work. At Elizabethport it built a crossover railroad that took people to the Jersey Shore with stops at Elizabeth Avenue, Spring Street (U.S. Highways 1 and 9), Bayway, Tremley, Elmora, and every little town to Bay Head.

The Civil War moved Elizabeth into the Industrial Revolution. Prior to the war, there were small forges and foundries to make cooking stoves, furnaces, and other articles. There were lumber and coal yards, print shops, tanneries, shoe manufacturers, and small shipyards.

Numerous veterans' organizations were formed. They included the Grand Army of the Republic (GAR), an organization to perpetuate the principles for which they fought and provide charity for the sick and disabled soldiers and families; the Ulric

Dahlgren Post 25, Department of New Jersey, organized to place suitable gravestones on the graves of all soldiers and sailors and raise funds to assist the sick and needy servicemen; the U.S. Grant Post 93, composed mainly of the Veteran Zouaves; and the Judson Kilpatrick Post 64, composed of veterans of the War Between the States. There was also the Major David H. Hatfield Camp 1, New Jersey Division, Sons of Veterans, to keep green the memories of their fathers and aid the needy members of the GAR. This post appears to have been the only one with a Ladies' Auxiliary.

The Phil Kearny Guard, Company C., organized by Captain William H. DeHart, had a drill team that competed throughout the country. It was the only military unit present at the nation's centennial celebration in July 1876 in Philadelphia. DeHart was awarded the rank of brevet major in recognition of his 21 years of service with the drill team. Other veterans' groups include the Company E, Torbert Guard and Veteran Zouaves, Gatling Gun Company A, organized by General J. .Madison Drake.

A Civil War memorial committee was appointed to raise funds for a statue to those men who had fallen and those who had served in the great war. The site became Military Square on North Broad Street at Prince Street and Westminster Avenue in front of the Westminster Presbyterian Church. Although the fund drive began in 1865, it took until 1906 for the monument to be installed. The simple inscription states: "To the Soldiers and Sailors Who Fought to Preserve the Union, 1861–1865, Erected by the Citizens of Elizabeth, N.J. July 4, 1906."

A huge parade was interrupted by three thunder storms during the dedication of the monument. The climax of the ceremonies was reached not when the drape was pulled off the pedestal, but when a grandstand at the site collapsed. Fortunately nobody was injured.

These Pingry School boys are standing in front of the home of Jonathan Townley, whose house was used by the school while he served with the Union army during the Civil War.

5. The Golden Age and Bankruptcy 1866–1898

Although the people in the years after the Civil War were eager to embrace new industries, unaware of the hazards they might create, they still clung to their agrarian roots. The first New Jersey State Agricultural Society fair was held in Waverly Park near the Newark-Elizabeth line in 1867. Elizabethans and all their neighbors entered their prize horses, cattle, handiwork, fruits, vegetables, and preserves. Highlights of the four-day festival were the trotting races. Many gentlemen in the area competed in them. In addition to the exhibits there were amusements in the midway, and refreshments were served in "Little Germany."

The fame of the fair attracted President U.S. Grant on September 19, 1872, who arrived in a caravan of seven carriages. A correspondent of the new *Elizabeth Daily Journal* observed that President Grant was "received with vigorous devotion by the people." Grant was a frequent visitor to Elizabeth because his sister had married a local man, William Corbin.

The fair caused several hotels to be built along the new Frelinghuysen and Newark Avenues between Newark and Elizabeth to accommodate visitors. The most exciting guests however were the Gypsies who arrived in the area from the South each April and stayed until October, camping on a nearby island in their colorful wagons. The women told fortunes and the men traded horses. The people found the Gypsies a curiosity and enjoyed their presence. There were no reports of crime connected to them.

The agricultural society usually met in Elizabeth. The Waverly Fair continued to operate until 1900, when it was moved to Trenton and became the New Jersey State Fair. According to legend the name "Waverly" was given to the area by Mary Mapes Dodge, author of *Hans Brinker or the Silver Skates* and editor of *St. Nicholas Magazine*. She is reported to have loved the Waverley novels of Sir Walter Scott. A widow, she lived with her father James J. Mapes, who conducted an experimental farm on the Upper Road in Lyon's Farms for many years.

The fair grounds were adjacent to the area that became Weequahic Park, one of the two large Essex County parks within the City of Newark. The park borders Elizabeth and contains a large lake.

On April 1, 1869, the Union County Historical Society was incorporated by the 93rd Legislature of the State of New Jersey. Members whose names were listed in the incorporation papers included Orestes A. Brownson and John Gilmary Shea, both Roman Catholic theologians, writers, and editors; William Magie, a chancellor of New Jersey; Robert S. Green, a governor; Dr. Louis W. Oakley, a physician; William F. Day, a lawyer; and Frederick F. Foote, the newspaper editor and publisher.

Architects were busy designing houses and builders were busy constructing them after the four years of war had curbed building. Many large Victorian-type houses in the city were built in this period on large lots on tree lined streets such as South and North Broad Streets and Elizabeth, Rahway, Westfield, and Morris Avenues. They usually had wrap-around porches and towers. Large carriage houses were in back of the mansions for their horses and carriages. Sometimes there were additional buildings for chickens, tools, and greenhouses. There were flower gardens, flowering shrubs, and vegetable gardens, and one or two fruit trees. The entire plots were surrounded by wrought iron fencing. As the people became more prosperous they moved uptown.

One of these houses has been preserved by Elizabeth's Central Baptist Church. It is the Whyman house on Newark Avenue, with a wrought iron fence and water fountain, barn, and other outbuildings making it a self-contained house. It was donated to the church, which uses it as the parsonage.

Twenty-five women in the city were invited to the St. John's parsonage by Mrs. Samuel A. Clark, wife of the rector of St. John's Episcopal Church, to discuss formation of a Ladies' Book Club of Elizabeth in 1874. The group decided to meet in Library Hall in the Arcade Building. Dues were $3 a year and were used to

The Henry A. Rath Plumbing Company was at 1217 East Jersey Street in 1889.

purchase books. At first every member read every book. Arrangements were made for book repairs, donations of some of the books to the free public library, and gifts to various agencies. The secretary was responsible for the distribution of the books.

The St. Paul's Methodist Episcopal Church and the Elizabeth Avenue Methodist Episcopal Church, both begun just before the Civil War, united to form the St. James Methodist Episcopal Church. The combined churches purchased the former Baptist church on South Broad Street near the Stone Bridge. Services began in 1877. Reverend Henry Spellmeyer, pastor from 1878 to 1880 and a poet, subsequently became a missionary to China. The church flourished for more than 100 years, then the congregation dwindled and the church dissolved in 1994. Several ethnic congregations have met in the education building since the Methodist church closed. The Park Methodist Episcopal Church opposite Jefferson Park on Madison Avenue was built in 1875. It became a child care center at the close of the twentieth century.

New churches were built to meet the demands of the growing populations as the city spread out. Trinity Episcopal Church built a small building at East Jersey Street and Jefferson Avenue in 1860, which was sold. It conducted services at the Third Presbyterian Church until a new building on North Broad Street at Chestnut Street was dedicated in 1866, the same year that the Westminster Presbyterian Church was formed on North Broad Street.

The Westminster church was formed by the Second Presbyterian Church to serve people who lived above the Union Railroad Station, then considered a stylish section of the city. Reverend William C. Roberts, pastor of the Second Presbyterian Church, was called to be pastor of the Westminster church, and served until 1881. The brownstone church with its two towers was dedicated in 1876. Reverend James Paterson became pastor at Second church when Reverend Roberts left it. Reverend Dr. John Gillespie followed him in 1882, serving until 1886, when Reverend Dr. John W. Teal accepted the call.

The East Baptist Church was dedicated in September 1871 on Third Street as a memorial to the daughter of Peter B. Amory. It was disbanded in 1879 and reorganized the following year. The church had several names before it was moved to Clark at the circle for the Garden State Parkway and joined the Union County Baptist Church.

Prior to the Civil War, African Americans attended the same churches as the rest of the population. The roots of the Mount Teman African Methodist Episcopal Church on Madison Avenue were in a church begun in 1830. It was disbanded. In 1860, the Mount Teman African Methodist Episcopal Church was organized. The Certificate of Corporation was not signed, however, until 1884. The congregation met at several locations including the original site of St. Mary's Roman Catholic Church on Washington Avenue and a tiny building erected by the congregation at 16–18 South Union Street, used until 1967. Plans were made for a new sanctuary during the pastorate of Reverend Walter Wayman Clark. The edifice was erected at 166 Madison Avenue in 1967. The congregation formed a procession to walk from South Union Avenue to Madison Avenue for the church dedication. Normally pastors serve two years in the church. During the time Reverend Jesse J. Jackson was pastor, six youths in the church became ministers. It is believed to be the oldest African-American congregation in Elizabeth.

The First Presbyterian Church organized the Siloam Presbyterian Church for African Americans in the Session House on Dickinson Street in 1867, and in 1873, African-American members of the Baptist Church formed the Fourth Baptist Church in Library Hall on Broad Street. It closed. The Shiloh Baptist Church at 95 Murray Street was formed in 1879, by the Negro Baptist Congregations of New Jersey. It met first at the home of James E. Connick in Union Street and then at Collette Hall, located at 100 Broad Street. The property on Murray Street was purchased in 1894. The present building was erected in 1923.

The Burger Leather Company began in Elizabeth in 1863. Initially it was located at 1172 Elizabeth Avenue and made saddles for horses. From 1940 to 1950, when it closed, the company made leashes and collars for dogs. Three generations of the Burger family worked in the company. Councilman John M. Burger established the business during the Civil War. His son John E. Burger followed him. His grandson John F. Burger closed the business in 1950.

Although many Germans, Irish, Scotch-Irish, and Scottish migrated to Elizabethtown by the 1840s, the brewing of beer was a home operation. The first commercial brewery, the Eller and Bayer Company, opened in 1864. It was purchased by Peter Breidt in 1882 and became the Peter Breidt City Brewing Company at 900 Pearl Street, the present site of the Elizabeth High School. The company operated only until 1920, when the Volstead Act became effective, outlawing all liquor. The Southern Sash and Sales Company used the building before it was torn down for the school.

Only one other brewery was operated in the city. This was the Seeber Brewery Company, started in 1887. It was operated by three generations of the Seeber family. It also was known as the Rising Sun Brewing Company and was located on Marshall Street. After it closed in 1920, it was used as a syrup company, fabrics house, produce warehouse, and a bar supply warehouse.

In 1871, Frederick W. Foote, a former teacher who began publishing and editing the *New Jersey Journal* in 1863, started the *Elizabeth Daily Journal*, a six-day a week paper. The *New Jersey Journal* continued as a weekly until 1890, when the two papers were merged. The paper moved twice while Foote owned it with a partner: first James S. Drake from 1863 to 1870, and then Edward H. Clement from 1871 until 1897. The paper's office was on the southeast corner of Broad and East Jersey Streets until 1888, when it moved across the street to 72–74 Broad Street, next to the National State Bank.

The Elizabeth Ice Company was started in 1866 by Ross & Reeve, and two years later the firm was Reeve & Williams. Nineteen years later it was incorporated as the Elizabeth Ice Company. M.W. Reeve was listed as president, C.H.E. Halsey was secretary-treasurer, and R.S. Williams was superintendent. The ice house was located on the shore of Ursino Lake on the Elizabeth-Union border and the ice was cut from the lake. In 1889 Frederick F. Glasby, whose ice house was on

Madison Avenue, became the company's competitor when he cut ice in Lake Hopatcong and hauled it to Elizabeth during the winter for storage.

Religious institutions became more diversified after the Civil War as the population grew and migrants arrived from Southern and Central European countries as well as Sweden. The Westminster Presbyterian Church organized the Madison Avenue Presbyterian Church in 1873, to serve the area between Jefferson Park and North Park (now Kellogg Park). The Third Presbyterian Church organized the Westminster Hope Chapel in 1874. By 1885, the chapel was placed under the care of the Westminster Presbyterian Church. It later became Hope Presbyterian Church on Spring Street. The German Presbyterian Church began in Elizabethport in 1879. Reverend Dr. Eben B. Cobb followed Reverend Hugh Smythe (1877–1885) as pastor of the Second Presbyterian Church from 1877 to 1925.

The railroads made the people of Elizabeth realize that they needed street transportation to travel from one section of the city to another. Horse railways were introduced. The cars were shaped like railroad cars but were pulled by one or two horses. The first routes were short and sometimes a person would have to take several trolleys to reach his destination. Gradually the routes were extended. Among them were the Elizabeth and Newark Horse Railway Company; the Connelly Street Railway Equipment Company, formed in 1866; and the Elizabeth Street Railway Company, incorporated in 1888. Gas motors began replacing horses in 1889, and soon they were electrified. When his boss wanted a new place

The Peter Breidt City Brewing Company started as the Eller and Bayer Company in 1864. It closed on January 1, 1920, when the Volstead Act prohibited the sale of alcoholic beverages. The site was purchased by the city in the early 1970s for the new Elizabeth High School.

to construct a factory, Lebbeus Baldwin Miller immediately suggested the home of his ancestors: Elizabeth, New Jersey. Thus it was that Isaac Singer, owner of the Singer Manufacturing Company, makers of home and industrial sewing machines, purchased 32 acres of land on Newark Bay in Elizabeth.

The first sewing machine was invented in England by Thomas Saint about 1790, to stitch shoes and boots. Elias Howe Jr. produced a machine in 1846 to sew cloth, but it would only sew a few stitches at a time. By 1850, Isaac M. Singer of Boston, a mechanic, developed the first workable sewing machine when he sewed five continuous stitches at once. He patented the lock stitch machine in 1851 and continued to work on the machine to increase both its speed and the number of stitches it could sew. Edward Clark, a lawyer, represented Singer in a suit by Elias Howe Jr., who claimed Singer had infringed on his patent rights in development of a wood carving machine Singer invented in 1849. Clark won the case for Singer and offered to represent the company in its legal affairs for ten years in exchange for a partnership. Singer agreed. The company became I.M. Singer & Company with Clark as the "Company." He later became the firm's second president.

The sewing machine company relocated to New York City and became the Singer Manufacturing Company in 1863. Because operating the factory in the heart of the city was expensive, the owners sought a cheaper location. Miller was employed by Singer at the time and recommended Elizabethport. The company relocated to a new factory in the Port in 1873, and the plant seemed to grow by leaps and bounds as it sought to keep pace with the demands for the machines. Clark is credited with building up the company by introducing installment payments, trade-in allowances to buy new machines, and a rental-purchase plan for individuals, all still in use today.

The industrial sewing machines gave employees in factories throughout the area shorter hours and regular pay envelopes. They made it possible for one woman operating a foot-powered machine to do the work of 20 women sewing by hand. The sewing machine changed the clothing industry from the homemaker who laboriously sewed dresses or the dressmaker who visited a family for a week or so each season to make new dresses for the women and children.

Besides reducing the time to make clothes, the machines reduced the cost of clothing and made it possible for women to have more. It also standardized sizes, so patterns could be made for these clothes. Women began to purchase clothes off the rack in stores instead of making them at home or going to a dressmaker. Clothing stores developed and carried an assortment of styles for every taste and size.

In addition to making clothes, the housewives could also make curtains, suits, pillows, and other household necessities with less effort than before. The machines also expanded a woman's way of making a living, supplementing the family's income or acquiring some money of her own by permitting her to do piece work for a textile company at home without leaving her children.

A $125 sewing machine represented about one-fourth of a family's annual income in the 1880s. Despite this the Singer factory was turning out 3,000 machines weekly. "The company" became *the* place to work, especially for craftsmen. The work capacity grew to 1,500 machines daily. The company constantly sought to improve its product. It introduced motor-driven sewing machines for clothing factories in 1889, and smaller electric machines for the home to replace the paddle-powered ones. Portable machines were developed for persons with limited space to store them when not in use. Wood cabinets were made for the machines so that when they were not being used, they would appear to be occasional tables in a hallway or a room.

The growth of the Singer plant was phenomenal. Soon it covered 113 acres and had 52 buildings. It became the largest employer in Elizabeth, and some say the world. In the beginning a spur of the Central Railroad of New Jersey ran through the yard to carry sewing machines from Elizabeth across the nation by freight cars. Railroad tracks extended throughout the complex delivering metal, wood, and other materials for the machines. *The Edward Clark*, the company's steamer, carried completed machines across Newark Bay to markets in New York City.

Many people and entire families worked in Singer for their entire working lifetimes. Children and even grandchildren of employees followed them into the company. For a time, everyone in Elizabeth appeared to have at least one family member employed there.

Philip Diehl, a German inventor, joined the Singer Manufacturing Company to find ways to improve the product. He developed several electrical products to improve the machines. In 1885, he formed the Diehl Company to manufacture electric motors. He continued to do research and development for Singer for the rest of his life.

William H. Rankin, who operated a roofing and sheathing works on South Street and Water Street (Elizabeth Avenue), started his business in 1873. He

Lawyer Edward Clark was the second president of the Singer Manufacturing Company from 1876 to 1882. A recreation center was built near the factory for company employees and named for Clark.

manufactured sheathing, roofing pitch, liquid roof paint, roofing, and other items, many invented or improved by him. He built a brick residence adjacent to the factory for his employees. Many of his products were exported, especially to South America. Unfortunately, the Panic of 1873 swept across the nation, halting many of these activities. Among these was homebuilding on large improved lots in Elizabeth. The City anticipated assessing the new homeowners for paved streets, sewers, and sidewalks after the houses were erected instead of before they were built. The panic caused the rapid building of dwellings to cease. By 1878, the City was forced to declare bankruptcy because it was unable to pay for these improvements on the still vacant land.

Thomas A. Edison lived at 235 Morris Avenue in Elizabeth from September 12, 1869 to April 23, 1870, while he operated his first factory in Newark. He then opened a research laboratory in Menlo Park until 1882, when he moved to West Orange. While in Menlo Park, he obtained 300 patents. His first electric generating plant was erected in Roselle, adjacent to Elizabeth, in 1878, where 35 dwellings, the original chandelier in the First Presbyterian Church in Roselle, and Charlie Stone's store in Roselle Park were lighted by electricity.

Construction of the Elizabethport and Perth Amboy Railroad, later known as the Perth Amboy Railroad, began in the spring of 1871. The railroad joined the Central Railroad of New Jersey at Elizabethport and extended to Long Branch in June 1875 and finally Bay Head, opening the Jersey Shore area to the Elizabethans. Another branch of the railroad went into Broad Street, Newark.

Freight trains on the Jersey Central line went through the Singer yard on Newark Bay and sent cargo to New York City about 10 miles away. *The Chancellor*, owned by the railroad, made two round trips daily to New York carrying manufactured products from Elizabeth. Connections with ports along the Atlantic Ocean, its bays and rivers, or inland waterways such as the Erie Canal could be made easily. Elizabeth soon earned the nickname "The Rail and Harbor City."

Meanwhile, the immigrants kept arriving in Elizabethport from Europe. Polish immigrants began moving into Elizabeth in the 1870s. They organized St. Peter & Paul Lithuanian Church in Elizabeth and attended it until St. Adalbert, named for the patron and apostle of Poland, could be organized in 1905. Both groups worked at the Singer plant. Soon both churches had their own parochial schools and organizations. Ethnic bakeries and markets grew near the churches. By 2000, the population in Union, Essex, and Hudson Counties numbered about 5,000 Lithuanians. Many of them continued to travel to St. Peter and St. Paul. The number of people of Polish descent is listed at 200,000, but most of them have moved to the suburbs.

American Gas Furnace Inc., now AGF Inc., manufacturers of industrial gas heat treatment furnaces, burners, and appliances, was founded in 1878 on Route 1 or Spring Street. It was a division of Mapes and Sprowl. It continues today to supply the same service in a well-kept vintage factory building.

The T.F. & H.C. Sayre Company began in 1879 selling masons' building materials such as blue stone, lime, and cement from its site between the Elizabeth

The Elizabeth General Hospital was known as the City Hospital when it opened in 1879. It is now part of Trinitas Hospital.

River and Elizabeth Avenue. The Eugene Munsell & Company at Fulton and Marshall Streets made heating and cooking stoves, furnaces, fireplaces, and portable ranges. Graff & Company on Elizabeth Avenue moved to Elizabeth in 1884 to manufacture furnaces and oven ranges. L.B. Beerbower or Elizabeth Pottery manufactured common red earthenware from clay from the banks of the river just as Keen Pruden did.

Edmund Clarence Stedman (1833–1908) lived in Elizabeth for 14 years from 1854 to 1868. During that time he worked for the *New York Tribune* when it was guided by Whitelaw Reid, and wrote his first volume, *Poems, Lyric and Idyllic*, which was published in 1860. He was a correspondent for the newspaper during the Civil War until poor health caused him to leave. When the war ended, he acquired a seat on the New York Stock Exchange. His second book, *Alice of Monmouth and Other Poems*, appeared in 1863. After four more volumes of poetry, he wrote *The Library of American Literature* with Ellen M. Hutchinson in 1890, and a critical comment on "The Works of Edgar Allan Poe" with Professor George E. Woodberry in 1895. These were followed by his *Victorian Anthology* in 1895, and his *American Literature* in 1899. His poetry has been forgotten, but his criticism has endured. His mother Elizabeth Clementine Dodge Stedman Kinney, also a poet, married William Burnet Kinney, editor and publisher of the *Newark Advertiser*. Through them Stedman met the literary circle in Newark, which included Mary Mapes Dodge, author of *Hans Brinker or the Silver Skates*.

The Cooke Brothers, established in 1880 on South Fourth Street near the Baltimore and Ohio Bridge, made lard, tallow, and oils for soap and candlemakers.

The Bowker Fertizer Company just south of the bridge made fertilizers. Sheridan's Mill on Broad Street beside the site of the old Stone Bridge made blinds, doors, and sash, while C.C. Pierson on Pennsylvania Avenue made ladders.

The City of Elizabeth was without a hospital until 1879, when Dr. Alonzo Pettit and his wife Ellen M. Dimock Pettit, a member of the Dimock family whose dwelling became the first Battin High School, established the Pettit Training School for Nurses as a hospital. It became Elizabeth General Hospital, later Elizabeth General Medical Center and now part of Trinitas Hospital.

Anthony W. Dimock built his mansion in the 1870s. He suffered business reverses in the stock market crash of 1873 and sold the mansion to Joseph Battin, who purchased it and in turn gave it to the City of Elizabeth on March 15, 1889, for use as a high school. It was replaced in 1913 by the present structure. Dimock's son, also an Anthony, wrote *How to Become A Millionaire by Twenty-One*, which is just what he did. He subsequently wrote boys' books, worked as a stockbroker, a photographer, and a naturalist.

When General Winfield Scott taught at the U.S. Military Academy at West Point after his failed attempt to lead the Union forces at the start of the War Between the States, one of his associates was Colonel Dennis Hart Mahan, who taught engineering. After Mahan's death, his widow Mary Helena Okill Mahan moved her family to 232 South Broad Street in 1871. Mrs. Mahan was a relative of John Jay, who had married Sarah Livingston. She was accompanied to the city by her son Alfred Thayer Mahan, who became a famous naval historian, and by at least one daughter. The family occupied the home until the 1940s.

Alfred Thayer Mahan became a naval officer and discovered he hated sea duty because every time he boarded a ship he was sea sick. He sought shore duty, but the navy kept sending him to serve on the U.S.S. *Pocahontas* and the U.S.S. *Seminole*, which were assigned to blockade duty along the Confederate coast during the Civil War, the U.S.S. *Wachusett*, the U.S.S. *Chicago*, and the U.S.S. *Iroquois*, which took him to England, Europe, the Mediterranean Sea, South America, and Asia.

Mahan also is said to have suffered from severe headaches and skin disorders. To escape, he read history and romantic novels while he attended Annapolis. As he grew older he became interested in naval battles. This interest was accelerated in 1885 when he was asked to lecture on tactics and naval history at the U.S. Naval War College in Newport. His first lecture was delayed until 1886, when he also was named president of the college, a post he held until 1889. He collected his lectures and published them in a book in 1890, *The Influence of Sea Power Upon History, 1660 to 1783*. The book is considered one of the most significant published during the nineteenth century. It was studied by the military leaders in Russia, Japan, England, and Germany, and influenced military leaders and politicians in the conduct of the Spanish-American and Russo-Japanese Wars, and World War I.

Joseph Gale, a *Newark Evening News* reporter, in his book, *Eastern Union County, The Development of a Jewish Community*, notes two synagogues on South Park Street for Orthodox Jews. They united and became Holche Yosher Synagogue. The synagogue also started a cemetery of its own as was the custom at that time. It was one of 14 placed along McClelland Street on the Elizabeth-Newark line. The synagogue built Library Hall in the Port, which was used for Hebrew and Christian religious services and community group meetings for many years. Congregation Israel, another Orthodox synagogue, also was formed.

While men usually worked 12-hour shifts six days a week, there was still time for fun on Sundays. There were baseball games, beer gardens, bicycle clubs, and boating. The Elizabeth Athletic Club had a clubhouse on West Grand Street equipped with an indoor gym with apparatus, a billiard room with four tables, reading room, and four bowling alleys. It was organized in February 1878. There also were provisions for track racing and boxing. The Alcyone Boat Club formed in 1872 and conducted rowing races on the Arthur Kill. It competed with rowers from the Kill van Kull Rowing Association. The Arthur Kill Rowing Association formed in 1878 and built a boat house at the foot of East Jersey Street. The Viking Rowing Association was the oldest rowing group in the area, starting in 1873 with the uniting of the Elizabeth Boat Club and the Triton Boat Club. A new clubhouse was built at Bayonne and all boats were moved to it.

A swing bridge, the first to Staten Island from New Jersey, was built in 1887 for the 5-mile long Staten Island Transit Railroad, a short railroad line from the Central Railroad of New Jersey at Cranford through a portion of Roselle, Linden, and Elizabeth across the Arthur Kill to St. George on Staten Island. The transit railroad was formed in 1881, after an agreement was approved with the Baltimore and Ohio Railroad. The new bridge was 498 feet in length with an 83-foot approach from the west and an 147-foot approach from the east. It was known as a "single track through-truss pivot swing central span" bridge. It only had one connection with another railroad, the Pennsylvania, at Linden Junction.

On March 11, 1888, it began to snow. The snow continued for more than two days, and trains on the railroad were forced to halt. Passengers were stranded in cold railroad cars. The horses and pedestrians had difficulty walking through the deep drifts. Activities in the city ceased. Stores were unable to open. The few that did because the proprietors lived on the property soon closed because no customers came. Food and coal could not be delivered. A few sleighs pulled by Morgan-type horses were able to get through the streets. But they were rare. The city was without power equipment and was unable to dig itself out. Finally on March 13, the snow stopped and the temperature rose. The Blizzard of Eighty-Eight was dubbed the worst in the area's history. It provided fodder for newspaper stories for a century and stories for senior citizens who were children when the snow fell.

In April 1889, there was a grand observance of the centennial of President-elect Washington's trip through Elizabeth to become the first president of the United States. President Benjamin Harrison was the stand-in for Washington for the occasion. Instead of arriving by coach or on a white horse, he descended from a Pennsylvania Railroad train at the Union Station at 7:25 a.m. and was greeted by

Mayor Joseph Grier (1883–1890). The reception committee also included Reverend F.M. McAllister, rector of Trinity Episcopal Church, Representative Amos Clark, Charles Russ, and state officials. Every church bell in the community was rung and cannon roared. President Harrison was escorted to the home of Governor Robert Stockton Green on the corner of West Jersey and Cherry Streets, where breakfast was served. Decorations included American flags and cut spring flowers. The china service owned by Governor Green's great-grandfather Robert Stockton, the first chaplain of the U.S. Congress and a brother of Richard Stockton, signer of the Declaration of Independence, was used.

When breakfast was finished, the group went to the drawing-room where a reception was conducted for national, state, and local officials and organizations such as the state senate and assembly, former governors, members of the Society of Cincinnati, Sons of the American Revolution, the New Jersey Historical Society, the Washington Society, trustees and professors of the College of New Jersey, Princeton, and Rutgers College, the Union County Board of Chosen Freeholders, the Common Council, and many others.

The guests then went to a grandstand erected for the purpose to witness a grand parade of more than 3,000 people with Charles H.K. Halsey as the grand marshal. Veterans of the Civil War, the National Guard of New Jersey, fraternal organizations, and men representing various occupations composed the paraders.

Congregation B'nai Israel was founded on May 25, 1872. The Orthodox congregation worshiped in a rented hall until a synagogue was built in 1883. This building was dedicated in 1924 as a Reform congregation.

President Harrison then traveled by open carriage to the Arthur Kill under three arches and passed throngs of people who lined the street to the Alcyone Boathouse. The first arch was at Broad and Jersey Streets, the second at Union Square, and the third at First Street. The Union Square Arch was a living arch of steps and smiling girls, all dressed in white and each representing one of the states. Each girl held a bouquet of flowers. When the president's carriage reached the second arch, he took off his hat, stood, and smiled at the girls who showered his carriage with flowers. Upon reaching the Arthur Kill, President Harrison boarded a barge for the trip to New York. One observer said he feared the dock at the boathouse would sink because so many people crowded onto it. The barge was accompanied by a flotilla of boats.

Elizabeth was experiencing traffic jams long before the automobile or even the trolley car came into general use. The placement of Union Station for the two railroads just off Broad Street and Morris Avenue was a wonderful position for the traveler, but a hazard for the pedestrian or vehicle attempting to travel by the station. As the train service increased and the city grew, there were more and more carriages, carts, wagons, horses, trolley cars, and trains. When a train passed through on the tracks, all the traffic on Broad Street was blocked. Nothing could move. If the train stopped the delay increased. Businessmen who had stores along the street or people who wanted to travel along the street complained. Something had to be done to eliminate the bottleneck.

Finally it was decided to build an arch where Broad and North Broad Streets meet. The Pennsylvania Railroad was elevated and the Central Railroad was at ground level. In order to accomplish this, the roadway at the junction of the two streets was lowered 8 feet. The excavation put entrances to buildings on Broad Street at second-floor level. Amos Clark Jr., representing the property owners, filed a suit against the Central Railroad for damages to the property. He was opposed in court by William Corbin, another local attorney, representing the railroad. In the settlement that followed, Clark and his clients received funds to place entrances at the former basement levels. The Pennsylvania Railroad was not involved in the suit because its tracks were elevated over the Central tracks. The low area at the junction of the two streets flooded and a municipal pumping station was built nearby to prevent the accumulation of water.

Bicycles and bicycle clubs became popular in the 1890s. Several local firms began building them to fill the demand. Among them were Joseph B. and H.R. Benedict Brothers, the Curtis Cycle Company, the Eldredge Bicycle Company, the Elizabeth Manufacturing Company, F.E. Norris and Company, Smith and Walter, the Darby Cycle Company, the Gilbert and Chester Company, Farley S. Taylor, and Joseph Von Rhein, whose "Von" is missing in some city directories. Twenty years later only bicycle dealers and repair facilities were listed.

The "wheels" as they were called had fancy names such as Sternas, The Syracuse, the Barnes, Eldredge Pierce, Adlake, Sterling, Terbane, Columbo, Iver Johnson, Ariel, Andre, Monarch, Trinity, Falcon, Kenting, Carlisle, and the New Haven. Bicycle clubs were formed and bicycle tours taken. The name tour was used in place of race. A contestant would travel the race course several times before the appointed meet to become familiar with the route. The races might be 25 miles long and were conducted between Elizabeth and Newark. "The Century" was another tour. It extended 50 miles from Elizabeth and 50 miles back for the return trip. Several wheelmen clubs were formed. One of these was the Elizabeth Wheelmen, who had a clubhouse at 1203 East Broad Street.

One hot day a young couple stopped in Philip Mohr's confectionery store at 80 First Street. The young woman complained that the seltzer was not cold enough, and Mohr suggested putting some ice cream in it. She agreed, and the ice cream soda was born!

For most people, the tornado that carried Dorothy to the Land of Oz was just a spectacular beginning for a much-loved story. For the people in the center of Elizabeth on August 2, 1899, it was very real. According to witnesses, it was just another hot August day. The air was still, but at 3:00 p.m. a savage wind came up. It was followed by a severe thunder and lightning storm that caused most people to seek shelter in their homes or nearby stores. Shortly after the storm began, a funnel-shaped cloud swooped down to earth toppling the 212-foot spire of the First Presbyterian Church with its town clock, knocking over stones in the adjacent graveyard, uprooting century-old trees, and opening graves. It broke windows and pulled various possessions out of houses, overturned a delivery wagon of J. Potts and Sons, knocked over displays in front of drygoods and grocery stores, and carried away roofs of the Star and the Lyceum Theaters. Display signs and awnings were torn from their hinges.

The swirling cloud rose and descended on St. John's Episcopal Church, ripping slates from its roof, and skipped along East Jersey Street, damaging the steeple of the Central Baptist and the roofs of the Third Presbyterian and Christ Episcopal Churches. It blew down a black walnut tree that crashed into the house of Dr. Robert J. Montfort at 1051 East Jersey Street, and it damaged the Home for Aged Women, then located in Boxwood Hall. The greatest damage was done to dwellings on William and Catherine Streets where houses were cut in half, porches were blown away, and windows were torn out. A lineman for the Suburban Electric Company, working on the roof of Warren H. Dix's home (the Belcher-Ogden mansion) is said to have caught another workman in a second story window as he was blown off the roof and was falling toward the ground. The storm left as suddenly as it arrived.

The miracle of the twister is that nobody was killed. A few people suffered minor injuries. Police were called to prevent souvenir hunters and looters from stealing from the damaged buildings. The property owners were dismayed when they discovered that their buildings were not insured for tornadoes and they would have to pay for the repairs.

The steeple at the First Presbyterian Church was replaced and rededicated on October 11, 1901. A Citizens' Committee headed by H. Heywood Isham, Colonel Dennis F. Collins, and Judge P. Hamilton Gilhooly raised funds to replace it.

Meanwhile the city council was working hard to pay off its debts so that the city would regain its good reputation. Additional mayors during this period included Philip Grier, 1862–1871; William A. Coursen, 1873–1875; Robert W. Townley, 1875–1878 and 1879–1880; James S. Green, 1878; John C. Rankin Jr., 1890–1898; and Dr. William A.M. Mack, 1898–1901.

In the years between 1870 and 1900, Elizabeth's population increased from 10,832 persons to 52,130 people, according to the U.S. Census. Elizabeth, once a community with two sections: Elizabethtown and Elizabethport, now was a city with several sections. Each new subdivision had a new name such as Brittan Villa, Elmora, Westminster, or Quality Hill. Some names stuck, such as Bayway near the refineries, Peters018wn, or the Berg for the Italian section around Bryant Park, the Port for the area between Seventh and Fifth Streets and York Road and Livingston Street, and Froghollow from Atlantic Street north to Elizabeth Avenue and west to First Street. Others such as the West End, southside of the Central Railroad tracks and west of Elmora Avenue; the North End, Wilder Street and North Broad Street; and Routledge along Stanton Avenue to Kilsyth Road to Cross Avenue have faded away.

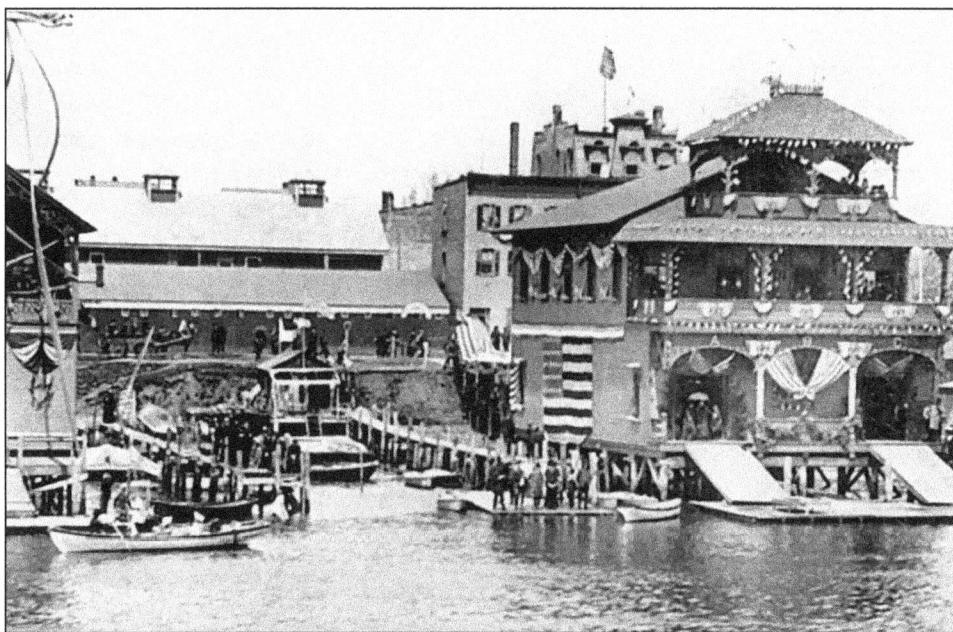

The Alcyone Boat Club was decorated for the visit of President Benjamin Harrison on April 29, 1889 and the reenactment of President-elect George Washington's trip to New York City in 1789.

6. GROWTH AND PROSPERITY 1899–1928

General George Washington ordered the people of Elizabethtown to build shallow draft boats during the Revolution. As far as we know they were built. During the years that followed the war, several businesses along the Arthur Kill and Newark Bay were devoted to the repair and operation of boats, and to some boat building. The Rutan, Colon & Crowell firm moved from Newark to the Elizabeth River in 1849. Sixty-four vessels were built by Colon in his lifetime. After Captain William Kachkart of Atlantic City built the *Matagorda*, a three-masted schooner at the yard in 1849, the Rutan, Colon & Crowell firm built *The Old Dominion*, also a three-masted schooner, and two others. Shipbuilding appears to have stopped after the Civil War except for repairs of vessels already at sea. Major repairs were done by the S.L. Moore & Son Company known as "The Crescent Iron Works" and the New Jersey Dry Dock Company.

Elizabeth became a major ship building community and almost became the center for the manufacture of automobiles, trolley cars, and airplanes as the twentieth century began. Several vessels for Mexico and other nations were built at the Port. The young ladies of Elizabeth found the Mexicans most exciting because they sent a group of young Mexican naval officers to supervise the construction of *The Tempico* in 1900 and *The Vera Cruz* in 1901. The officers were entertained during their stay by the leading citizens of the city. Vessels also were made for the Russians.

The U.S.S. *Bancroft*, the U.S. Navy's first steel vessel, was built at Elizabeth's Crescent yard in 1892. It was named for George Bancroft (1800–1891), a noted historian from Worcester, Massachusetts. Two other vessels were named for him.

John Holland, a teacher in Paterson, New Jersey, made a 14-foot cigar-shaped submarine in 1878, tried it out in the Passaic River, and survived. The coffin-like container is on view at the Rogers Locomotive Museum in Paterson. His next vessel was 31 feet long and he stayed under water for an hour. Lewis Nixon of New York City, who had rented the Crescent yard in 1895, heard about Holland's efforts and sold the idea to the U.S. Government, which ordered Holland's third submarine, a 43-foot vessel. After trial runs in the Arthur Kill, the navy accepted

People crowd the platform of a local railroad station as troops prepare to leave to participate in World War I.

the Holland submarine and ordered more in 1903. The first sub was named the *John P. Holland* in honor of its inventor.

At least 100 vessels were built at the yards during this period. They included several shallow draft, heavily armored ships such as the U.S.S. *Monitor* used in the Civil War. The shipyard was sold first to the United States Ship Building Corporation in 1902, and then to the Bethlehem Steel Corporation in 1905. It was merged with the Bethlehem Ship Building Corporation in 1917, and became known as the Moore plant. Arthur Leopold Du Busc was manager of the Bethlehem Shipbuilding Corporation in 1917, during World War I. The company received an order from the U.S. government for 50 ships. They were completed by 1920. Among them were cargo ships, tugs, and tankers.

After 1920, shipbuilding ceased along the Arthur Kill. Only repairs were made to ships. After a quarter of a century of building large ships, Elizabeth's days as a shipbuilding port were over. When World War II approached, city officials were asked if shipbuilding would resume. An official answered that it would cost too much to put the yards back into order. The shore of the Arthur Kill was neglected until a yacht basin and small park were developed. The city officials plan to extend the park along the waterfront.

Elizabeth nearly became a major automobile manufacturing center as well. In 1899, Andrew Lawrence Riker built the Riker Electric Vehicle Company in the Port to make battery-powered automobiles. The factory operated for three years. Unfortunately the batteries had to be recharged regularly to operate. From time to

105

time whenever there is a gasoline shortage, manufacturers consider making these automobiles. Some experimental ones are on the road, including some electric-gasoline hybrid cars, but so far the idea has not interested the general public.

Some other automobiles were made in Elizabeth. They included the Dusenberg Motor Company, which manufactured several cars on Newark Avenue. The building was purchased by William C. Durant, one of the founders of General Motors Company, who made the Star and Flint cars. The company failed. The building became the Waverly Terminal Company and some 40 small industries were housed in it.

In the mid-1930s, the Big Bear, the first supermarket in the area, offered groceries and all sorts of other articles. In 1938, George Burry moved the Burry Biscuit Company to the terminal. This cookie company was purchased by Quaker. Oats Company in 1962, and then by Interbake Food Company, which continues to bake cookies.

The Standard Aircraft Company on Bayway Avenue made airplanes and operated the first air field in the area during World War I. The company sought an airmail contract. The first airplane crash in Elizabeth was of a Handley Page airplane built by the company in 1919, at the field.

The Elizabeth Young Men's Christian Association was started in 1901, because so many young men from farms or abroad arrived in Elizabeth and needed a place to live, eat, study, and play. The Y rented two floors above a drug store on Broad Street and then built the 1905 building on East Jersey Street with a swimming pool, gymnasium, and classrooms. A show with a cast of more than 200 participants tracing the history of the nation was presented by the Y members to raise funds for the building. The youths were taught to figure, prepare building plans, and perform certain exercises in the gymnasium. The building was soon outgrown.

The Benedictine Sisters opened the Bender Academy and a normal school for teacher training at Benedictine Academy, both in Elizabeth, in 1919. The first building was in the family home of Albert Bender, a lawyer, at 416 Linden Avenue, in honor of his father, the late Fire Commissioner Frederick Bender. The school was non-sectarian and opened with the first four grades only. The fee was $40 a year. Piano lessons were offered to all children for an additional $40. Later the school was rededicated to both of Mr. Bender's parents after his mother died. John F. Kenah, mayor from 1923 to 1932, and Judge Alfred Stein, delivered the addresses at the dedication of the new Bender Memorial Academy on September 11, 1927, at the same site. A few years later Mayor Kenah had to cope with the start of the Depression, non-payment of taxes by some overextended property owners, and bankruptcies of many businesses. Thomas Williams served as mayor in 1933 and 1934.

The Y purchased the Woodruff House on Madison Avenue for the new building erected in 1928. Sunday afternoons were devoted to religious services. Ministers came from New York City, Trenton, and other venues by train to preach. Girls and approved young women from Elizabeth were invited to dances at the Y. The Women's Auxiliary conducted many dinners as fund raisers to feed the members, residents, and guests.

The Westminster Presbyterian Church sponsored the Hope Memorial Church until it built a house of worship in 1893 on Spring Street. A larger building replaced it in 1913, and the name was changed to Hope Memorial Presbyterian Church in 1925. Reverend Dr. John B. Crowell was pastor of the church for 47 years from 1927 to 1974, longer than any other pastor in Elizabeth. Reverend Dr. William F. Hawkins Sr. was called to the Siloam Presbyterian Church in 1977, and served until his death in 1997. The Siloam Church united with the Hope Memorial Church in 1985.

St. Henry's Roman Catholic Church became Sacred Heart Roman Catholic Church in 1888. A new building was erected on Spring Street, the future U.S. Highway 1 and 9. In 1928, the highway was widened and the entire edifice was moved back from the road. Although started by Germans and named for a German priest, the church became known for its Irish congregation. When it appeared necessary, another Irish congregation, Blessed Sacrament Roman Catholic Church, was formed on North Avenue between Madison and Monroe Avenues. The present sanctuary was erected on Madison Avenue in the early 1960s.

Members of the Junior League of Elizabeth made plans for a fundraising fashion show in the 1920s during a meeting at McManus Brothers furniture store on East Jersey Street.

In 1902, the Ladies' Book Club moved to Carteret Arms where the Free Public Library was then located. Carteret Arms was an inn when Lafayette is reported to have danced on the lawn. Problems with times of meetings resulted in the books being moved to St. John's Chapel and the sale of all but 25 of the reserved books. Reverend Dr. W.S. Langford followed Reverend Dr. Clark as rector of St. John's Episcopal Church in 1875. During his ten years in Elizabeth, he spearheaded the free public library. The Ladies' Book Club spurned novels, believing that its "intention in selecting books is not merely to amuse, but while interesting to instruct and improve."

The St. Elizabeth Hospital began in the Revolutionary War home of General Matthias Williamson in 1904. It was operated by the Sisters of Charity for women only.

St. Adalbert's Roman Catholic Church was incorporated in 1905. The church was established after Elizabeth Polish people petitioned Reverend Witus J. Masnicki, pastor of St. Stanislaus Roman Catholic Church in Newark, requesting that the parish be formed. A meeting attended by about 1,000 people on May 21 verified the request. Land was purchased for the church from the city for a sanctuary and school. Construction began before the end of summer. The church opened in June 1906, and Reverend Masnicki became the first pastor. It was the center for Polish culture, dancing, bowling, and the Union County Polish supplementary school to teach children the Polish language and culture. Within 18 years there were 1,864 children in the school and work began on another building. The Filician Sisters provided the teachers from 1906 to the 1970s, when lay teachers replaced them.

In 1912, two major buildings were constructed in Elizabeth. Andrew Carnegie, the Scottish millionaire, provided money to erect the Elizabeth Free Public Library building on South Broad Street, while the U.S. Post Office purchased the former home of Emily Hornblower Williamson, granddaughter-in-law of Governor Williamson, moved it around the corner on Westfield Avenue for the Elks Clubhouse, and erected the Elizabeth Post Office on the site of the house. The Elks Lodge later moved to a new building on Cherry Street when the post office added an addition. The Church of Jesus Christ of Latter Day Saints occupied the Cherry Street building after the lodge ceased operating. The Carteret Arms was used by the Elizabeth Woman's Club and then by St. Elizabeth Hospital for office space until it was razed for a newer office building.

Several additional municipalities were formed around the turn of the twentieth century. They included Roselle Borough from Linden in 1894, Fanwood Borough from Fanwood Township in 1895, Mountainside from Westfield in 1895, New Providence Borough from New Providence Township (Berkeley Heights) in 1899, Roselle Park from Union in 1901, Garwood from Cranford in 1903, Kenilworth from Union and Cranford in 1907, Hillside from Union in 1913, and Winfield from Cranford in 1941. In 1908, Elmora, a real estate development that had attempted to operate independently, rejoined Elizabeth to obtain modern city improvements. The name Elmora was invented by the realtor who developed the

Ground was broken for the new post office on North Broad Street in 1912 on the site of Emily H. Williamson's home. Her home was moved around the corner and served as the Elk's Club until the post office was enlarged.

area. Elizabeth's new borders included Newark Bay with Bayonne in Hudson County on the other side, Linden, Roselle, Roselle Park, Union, Hillside, Newark, and the Arthur Kill with the Borough of Staten Island, part of the City of New York, only 500 feet away.

Two women made a difference in Elizabeth in this era: Arabella Halsey Miller and Mrs. Williamson. Miss Miller, who was known to the boys of the Port as "Miss Belle," spearheaded the formation of the Visiting Nurse Association and the Family and Children's Society about 1892. Both agencies continue to be active today. Miss Miller established the first health center for children in Elizabeth. She turned her family home into a hotel and boarding home and formed the Pioneer Club for young men. The clubhouse was located in the Port. Later the city named a housing development the Pioneer Homes in honor of the club. The Arabella Miller Recreation Center was named for her in 1997.

Mrs. Williamson visited the alms house on Snake Hill in the meadows near Jersey City and found that infants and young children were housed with the mentally ill. If they lived until they were 12 years old, their parents would take them and place them in factories where young children could move around easier behind the wheels of the machines that made textiles. The children were undereducated and underfed. Williamson promoted the passage of laws prohibiting child labor. She became interested in the State Prison in Avenel and again obtained laws for better treatment of the prisoners.

She lived across the street from Governor Foster M. Voorhees, who was senate president when he became acting governor on February 1, 1898 and served until October 18, 1898. He was elected governor in 1898 and served from 1899 to 1902. He gave his 323-acre family farm to New Jersey for the Voorhees State Park in Hunterdon County. The state subsequently purchased an additional 300 acres for the park, which is known for its striking views of the countryside, picnic areas at Hoppock Grove and Hill Acre tracks, hiking trails, and nature areas. The New Jersey Astronomical Association also operates a celestial observatory at the park.

The public grammar schools housed classes for the normal school, which was city operated. The two-year course was moved from school to school. In 1910, the Elizabeth Board of Education promised a teaching position to the young woman with the highest marks. Mary R. Malson, an African American, ranked highest in the class of 17 students. There was some debate, but the board kept its promise. Miss Malson became the first African-American teacher in the Elizabeth School system. She taught until 1927, when she married. Her daughter Caroline Rice became the librarian at Battin High School. Mrs. Rice also was the captain of the first African-American Girl Scout and Brownie Troops in Elizabeth, and a charter member of the Elizabeth Branch of the National Association for the Advancement of Colored People (NAACP) and was also on the board of directors of the YWCA.

The Benedictine Sisters opened the Benedictine Academy in 1915 in a house on North Broad Street and quickly realized that they needed trained teachers so that the academy could compare favorably with the public schools. Classes were conducted for the teachers before and after school, in the evening and during the summer. Soon Catholic University in Washington, D.C. added summer classes for the new Sisters College of Catholic University. The sisters also started several grammar schools in Elizabeth: Blessed Sacrament School in 1926, and St. Genevieve's School in 1927.

William M. Ashby, the first African-American full-time social worker in New Jersey, traveled through Elizabeth from Roselle daily on his way to his job as a waiter in a Newark restaurant while he attended college. He later received a degree from Yale University. He formed the Urban League of Union County in Elizabeth and served as its director from 1944 to 1953. Later he was director of the Essex County League in Newark for many years. He is considered to be one of the most outstanding civil rights leaders in the area.

Jitneys, or motorized buses, were introduced to Elizabeth in 1916. Passengers entered by a door in the rear just as in the old horse-drawn wagons. Regulations for the buses began when the jitneys were introduced. Before regulations, youths would find an old car, put a notice in the window, and pick up passengers and drive anywhere. Even legal jitneys went where the operator wanted them to go. If business was slow on the driver's usual route, he would go somewhere else to find more business. There was no limit to the number of jitneys that might be on the road at one time. The jitneys had no set schedule or route. Many of them had no insurance in case of accidents. Passengers had to change jitneys frequently because most of the distances they traveled were short. There were no transfers, so a relatively short ride could become expensive. Some historians claim that the jitneys were the start of taxicabs.

Gradually laws were introduced. The State Board of Public Utility Commissioners on March 17, 1916, limited the area serviced and motor bus routes. It also began to regulate the design and construction of the bus to insure the safety and comfort of the passengers. The bus industry grew rapidly. After 1926, the utility board was given jurisdiction over all bus routes in the state except those carrying children to school. The next year a uniform code was adopted.

The U.S. Census listed 73,409 people in Elizabeth by 1910, 95,783 people in 1920, and 114,589 in 1930, the highest number of people counted until 2000, when the population increased to more than 120,000 people. The population became more diversified after 1880, when people from Southern and Eastern Europe began to arrive. In addition to Polish and Russian Jews, there were Polish, Russian, Italian, Greek, Slavic, and Swedish people. After 1900 there were Turks and Armenians. E. Opper's painting of a fire engine on Broad Street shows a Chinese laundryman. There were several Chinese-operated laundries in the city.

Ethnic groups and the public schools began teaching English to the newcomers. People of the same nationality grouped together in various sections of the city. Peterstown, named for the Peters family that once operated a farm in the vicinity

The Elizabeth Public Library was built in 1912. This photograph was taken in the 1920s.

around Bryant Park, became the Italian section of the city. Bayway with its Polish Club and St. Hedwig's Church became Polish. Ripley Place with the St. Peter and St. Paul Lithuanian Catholic Church was settled by Lithuanians. South Park Street with two synagogues was Jewish. The Port Irish moved to North Elizabeth and the Germans stayed close to St. Michael's on Smith Street for many years. The twentieth century would gradually reduce the ethnic neighborhoods as the people became better educated, received higher salaries, began moving uptown or to the suburbs, and intermarried.

The anti-German feeling was very strong during World War I and after. It was felt especially in the German-language churches. The First German Presbyterian Church's membership fell from 333 people before the war to 118 in 1919. The church purchased land on Magie Avenue in 1927 for a new building, changed its name to the Elmora Presbyterian Church, and dropped the use of the German language in 1928. That year, the church elected its first women deacons. The congregation also approved construction of a new building, which was dedicated in 1936. Reverend Albert E. Wirth served the church from 1892 to 1906, and was recalled in 1919, serving until 1935. Reverend Franklin L. Artley became pastor in 1937, serving until 1959. He was followed by Reverend Theodore O. Granberg in 1959, and Reverend Janet MacGregor-Williams in the 1990s.

Augustus S. Crane was publisher of *The Elizabeth Daily Journal* in 1907, when George W. Swift became managing editor. Swift held the post until he retired in 1948. During his tenure, the new *Journal* building was erected on the site of

Dr. Victor Mravlag, Elizabeth mayor from 1909 to 1911 and again from 1913 to 1923, rides in an open touring car during a 1919 parade.

Governor Voorhees's home on North Broad Street at Chestnut Street in 1924. Swift's influence on the newspaper was lasting. The paper was very Puritanical in its stories and photographs. Nothing risque was allowed.

Dr. Victor Mravlag, who was mayor from 1909 to 1911, served as mayor again from 1913 to 1923. Dr. Mravlag was a physician and very independent. When he first arrived in Elizabeth, he gave his cards to expectant mothers. After he became mayor he enforced healthy activities. Once he stopped at a confectionery store and scolded the storekeeper for the water on the sidewalk from melting ice. He was mayor during World War I, in which 120 Elizabeth men were killed. Mravlag unveiled a plaque in Scott Park in their memory on July 4, 1920. Dr. Mravlag was also mayor when the city celebrated its return to solvency after paying off the debts incurred by the 1878 bankruptcy. Vice-president Calvin Coolidge participated in the celebration.

Two well-known city residents served as Union County sheriffs: Captain Robert J. Kirkland and George C. Otto, a butcher. Captain Kirkland was sheriff from 1908 to 1911. Before that, he was the pilot of excursion boats on the Hudson River and around New York City and commander of the Singer Sewing Machine Company's maritime fleet. Later he sold real estate and insurance and represented the old Fourth Ward on the Board of Education. Otto became sheriff in 1914, and served until 1917. He operated a wholesale paper company for a time and worked as an inspector for the Wilson Meat Company in New York. He was commended during World War I for registering "slackers" who failed to report for the draft. His only son, George C. Otto Jr., later became Union County surrogate.

Numerous ethnic churches were formed at this time. Among them were St. Nicholas Carpatha Russian at 672 Broad Street, St. Peter's and St. Paul's Russian Orthodox at 127–129 Third Street; St. Peter's and St. Paul's Greek Catholic (Slavic) Church at 11 Delaware Street; and St. Vladimir's Ukrainian Catholic Church at 303 Grier Avenue.

The Mother House of the Benedictine Sisters was moved to the home of Mary Van Deveer Davis at 851 North Broad Street in 1923, from St. Warburga's Convent on Magnolia Avenue at Reid Street, where it had been since 1868. The mansion was designed by the architect Stanford White. Earlier the property was owned by Dr. Joseph Cross, who died in 1874. It was sold in 1876 to J. Pierpont Morgan, who apparently never lived in Elizabeth.

The 1920s were a prosperous time for churches. Some rebuilt where they were. Some like the Congregational Church, the German Presbyterian Church, and the German United Methodist Church moved uptown to Elmora, following their congregations. Several new ones were formed, including St. Hedwig's Roman Catholic Church at 715 Clarkson Avenue in the Bayway Section to serve the large Polish population there in 1925, with 350 families. Reverend Venceslau Slawinski was the first pastor. The parish grew rapidly. By 1950, the church was serving about 900 city families. The Polish Hall was nearby. The construction of the New Jersey Turnpike caused the removal of parishioners' homes. A new school building for 300 children, a convent, and sanctuary were erected a short time later.

A monument was also placed in front of them in memory of the members of the congregation killed during World War II. In September 2002, the school was closed because of low enrollment. Many of the families that once supported the church had moved from the city. Union County College rented the school in the fall of 2002.

The Holy Trinity Methodist Church on Amity Street and Second Avenue began in 1920, to serve Italian Methodists. Later services also were conducted in Spanish. The German Lutheran Church changed its name to St. Mark's Lutheran Church, but continued to conduct its services in German. St. Joseph's Roman Catholic Church (Slavish) at 116 Division Street, moved to Linden and its property became St. Joseph's Service Center. A new sanctuary for the 23-year-old St. Anthony of Padua Roman Catholic Church was dedicated on Elizabeth Avenue on November 6, 1927, for a large Italian-American congregation. Its school opened in 1958.

The huge Bayway Terminal on Bayway Avenue at South Front Street on the Arthur Kill opened on October 11, 1927. It contained a modern baler, the only one of its kind in the North, and was able to handle more than 10,000 tons of cotton daily. The capacity of the buildings was 200,000 bales. The Arthur Kill was dredged to a depth of 26 feet at low tide. The shipside channel adjacent to the building was 100 feet wide. New types of whip hoists were used to lift the bales of cotton into the warehouse. An agreement was made with the Central Railroad of New Jersey on July 17, 1926, for a spur into the facility where some 150 freight cars could be handled in one day. The warehouse flourished, but only for five years. The Depression struck and rayon, the first of the synthetic materials, was introduced. The firm went into receivership. It was used for several purposes after 1933, including Goodyear Tire and Rubber Company, Western Electric Company, Monsanto Chemical Company, Phelps Dodge Corporation, and finally as a furniture warehouse. In the 1970s, Phelps Dodge moved to Norwich, Connecticut, after a strike in Elizabeth.

Elizabeth had its own orchestra in the 1920s. There also were numerous jazz bands or combos playing in the city. Regina Woody, a former dancer, came to the city with her husband Dr. McIver Woody after World War I to establish his medical practice. Mrs. Woody began writing for dance magazines after an injury and also wrote children's books. The Menuhin family lived in Elizabeth for several years when their children were young. Yehudi, the violinist, became world famous. His sisters Hephzibah and Yaitah were concert pianists.

The Union County Historical Society (UCHS) was revived in the early 1920s. Mary E. Alward, New Jersey's second woman lawyer and Union County's first woman lawyer, became the secretary. While she was UCHS secretary, two books were published: *The Proceedings of the Union County Historical Society, 1921–1923*, and *Proceedings of the Union County Historical Society, 1923–1934*. Among the contributors were Callahan J. McCarthy; Warren R. Dix, superintendent of schools; and C.A. Philhower and Arthur L. Johnson, superintendents of the Union County schools.

Augustus S. Crane served as office boy, cashier, treasurer, president, and publisher of The Elizabeth Daily Journal. *His son Fred L. Crane succeeded him after his death in 1923.*

Augustus C. Crane, who started as an office boy and became the editor and publisher of *The Elizabeth Daily Journal*, died on January 6, 1923. His son Fred C. succeeded him and served until August 15, 1949, when he too died. Augustus's grandson Robert C. Crane followed them, serving until 1959, when the newspaper was sold to the Ralph Ingersoll chain and became part of the Mid-Atlantic Newspapers, Inc. The new management changed the name to *The Daily Journal*.

The Ritz and Regent Theaters opened in 1928, to show movies. Vaudeville acts frequently were included between the double features. Many future comedians, dancers, and singers honed their skills by traveling on the circuit. Both theaters were palaces. The Ritz on East Jersey Street is restored to its original splendor and frequently has bands or singers; the Regent on Broad Street is now a store.

Belle V. Rube became Elizabeth's first policewoman in 1921. She worked out of uniform in the court and investigated crimes involving women. She lost her job in December 1925 when the City Council refused to fund her position. In 1978, four women officers were appointed to the force, the first appointments of women in 53 years.

In 1923, Kirkpatrick Marrow, the first African-American policeman in Elizabeth, was appointed to the police department. He served in the detective bureau, specializing in gambling and alcohol investigations. He is said to have urged Don Newcombe to try out for major league baseball. Don did. He attended Thomas Jefferson High School and was selected to the Elizabeth High School Hall of Fame. Marrow retired in 1950 and became a court attendant in the Essex County Courthouse.

Women's suffrage and prohibition both became effective in 1920. Reverend Antoinette Blackwell, the city's first woman minister, voted in 1920 for the first time. She served briefly as the pastor of the Unitarian Church on Westfield Avenue after a lifetime of seeking civil rights for women. She was 100 years old when she cast her first ballot.

Prohibition created several new commercial ventures, all illegal. Among them were rumrunning, bootlegging, and running speak-easies. It seemed that everyone who enjoyed an alcoholic beverage had his own special source. Sometimes it was from someone who made bathtub gin, other times it was good liquor smuggled in from Canada. Most of the time it was from ships 10 miles off the Jersey coast that supplied the bottles to the rumrunners in small crafts, who then attempted to reach a safe harbor without being detected by the U.S. Coast Guard. In at least one instance, beer was illegally brewed at the Old Rising Sun Brewery on Seventh and Marshall Streets. The Federal Prohibition Enforcement Agency raided the brewery and Agent John Finello was shot and killed by gangsters. Arrests were made but nobody was convicted for the murder. The illegal operation closed down.

Oddly enough, the Alexian Brothers at the hospital, a German order, made beer throughout Prohibition and the police never bothered them. It was said to be excellent beer.

This open-air summer trolley car had a cow catcher on its front. This photograph was taken c. 1900.

116

7. Depression, War, and Civil Unrest 1929–1968

The Charleston dancing so popular in the 1920s stopped on Black Thursday, October 14, 1929, when the New York stock market crashed. This ended the post-war prosperity and began the Depression. The song of the times became "Buddy, Can You Spare A Dime?" Part of the Depression was caused by the practice of purchasing stock on margin and, when called to pay for the rest of the stock, being unable to raise the money . Brokerage houses were saturated with orders to sell stocks. With few or no bids for the stocks, the selling orders were worthless.

The market continued to drop to a low 41.22 in the Dow Jones Industrials in 1932. It took 25 years before the Dow climbed back up to the pre-Depression level of 1929. The newspapers were full of stories about people who committed suicide by jumping out of windows because they had lost their fortunes. People caused runs on banks as they feared their savings would be wiped out. They stood in line and withdrew all their money and hid it under their mattresses. It was reported that people used the worthless stock certificates to wallpaper their homes.

One by one, then two by two and more, companies cut back by firing some employees or giving them 10 percent or more pay cuts. When these acts failed they closed. There was no unemployment insurance and unemployment increased. Families had to turn to families, friends, or strangers for help. Home owners lost their homes when they were unable to meet the mortgage payments and the banks foreclosed, or when they were unable to pay the taxes and the City seized them. Families doubled up with relatives. Beggars went house to house seeking handouts of money or food or employment as painters, gardeners, and handymen. There were a few soup kitchens and breadlines, but few regular places to eat regularly. Men who once held good positions sought out unknown people in the telephone book, fraternity membership, or college or club yearbooks to seek positions from them. Few could be found.

Men with college educations unable to find employment in their fields became waiters, gasoline station attendants, or even street sweepers. They would do anything to earn money to place food on their tables. In Elizabeth, a jeweler who lost his store went to Sears to sell washing machines. A lawyer became a piano teacher. A French woman tutored school children in French. A man started making wooden lawn ornaments that he sold from his house, while another built a miniature golf course on his property.

Little girls who pressed their faces against the windows of department stores containing holiday displays learned not to cry for a Celluloid doll that cost only 10¢ because they realized early that 10¢ would buy a loaf of bread or a quart of milk for the family.

There were some success stories even during the Depression. Edward Stratemeyer, a native of Elizabethport, created a series of books for juveniles. The most popular was the "Nancy Drew" series. Others included "Tom Swift" and "The Bobbsey Twins." In each, he gave the author a pen name, the name of his hero, and an outline of the plot. Then he found college students, aspiring writers, or reporters to write the books. Although he died in 1930, the "Nancy Drew" series continues.

Donald Chidsey, one of Stratemeyer's young authors, began writing young adult history books about American subjects after he graduated from Princeton. Theodosia Pickering Garrison Faulks, a poet, wrote poems for women's magazines from about 1900 until her death in 1944. She wrote several books of poems, and some of her work appears in anthologies.

Elizabeth's movie theaters had bank nights. A person might win $5, $10, or even $25 if his name were called. They also gave out dishes. A woman patron would receive a dish each time she attended. If she went often enough she might manage to collect an entire set of dishes. If she dropped and broke a dish during a film everybody clapped and cheered. The theaters were handy places to keep warm, too. Admission to the balconies cost only 25¢ and the shows were continuous, with intermissions to clear out the patrons from the time the theater opened until it closed.

Dandelions were picked in the fields to make wine or salad by women. Some people began gardening on their own property, growing vegetables where flowers once were and preserving them for the winter. When men did go to stand in a relief line for food, they attempted to hide their faces so their neighbors or former fellow employees would not recognize them. Some went to the meadows between Newark and Elizabeth and built shacks from the materials on hand They would search the dump for materials to sell. They acquired seeds and planted them for food, which their wives would preserve for the coming winter.

More than one woman with a teaching degree returned to the classroom when her husband was unable to support the family. Until that time school systems hired only single women because it was felt that men could support their families. Usually they were paid less than their male counterparts. Many men, because of pay cuts in their regular jobs, sought part-time jobs to supplement their incomes. One Elizabeth teacher played in a band on weekends, while another worked part-time at a gasoline station.

John F. Kenah served Elizabeth as mayor from 1923 to 1932, from times of prosperity to the depths of the Depression.

The trolley or bus fare was only 5¢ per zone. An ice cream cone could be obtained for 5¢ also, and some ice cream sodas cost the high price of 15¢. Wages were low. A maid, frequently a German girl who arrived in the country after World War I, received only $30 a month. Weekly salaries of $15 to $18 were considered sufficient for shop girls, office clerks, and reporters. Teachers' salaries ranged from $1,000 to $2,600 in many systems. Lunches of a sandwich and soft drink could be purchased for 17¢ at Loft's, a chain restaurant.

Old newspapers were used by many people as substitute blankets to keep warm at night or under their clothes as a shield against the weather. People in Elizabeth took chances on a house that was raffled off in the Westminster Section with the hope that they would be the winner.

The Elizabeth Evening Times was a victim of the Depression in 1932. When it folded, Elizabeth became a one newspaper community with only one daily. Valentine A. Fallon transferred from the *Times* to the *Elizabeth Daily Journal* first as city editor and later the executive editor.

The People's Banking & Trust Company was sold in January 1935, at an auction to the Elizabeth Trust Company for $175,000 at St. Adabert's Roman Catholic Church because the Elizabethport branch of the bank lacked heat. It was just one bank that couldn't make it. Nationwide 4,004 banks closed in 1933 alone. One out of every four people in the nation was out of work.

The junior college movement began nationwide during the Depression. Union County College was opened in an old school in Cranford in 1933. Its Elizabeth branch began in 1991, in the former headquarters building of the Elizabethtown Gas Company Consolidated.

The Reichhold Chemical Company opened a plant on Bayway Avenue to produce surface coating synthetic materials in 1935. Pure resin is made from the barks of tropical trees and is very expensive. A synthetic resin was developed by Dr. Leo Baekeland in 1909, and was known as Bakelite. The synthetic resin was used on automobile steering wheels, telephones, and cameras. It also was used to make varnish that would not dissolve or melt. The resins dried rapidly and were durable. The Reichhold Company applied them to nearly every manufacturer of industrial finishes including the H.V. Walker Company.

The Civilian Conservation Corps (CCC) was formed to provide work on reforestation, soil erosion, flood control, road construction, and national park projects by young men 18 to 25 years of age. Soon work camps for the youths were erected throughout the countryside. The Works Progress Administration (WPA) was established two years later and probably is the better known organization. The WPA participants performed many of the same activities as the CCC, but stayed in their home area. In addition to construction projects, there were projects for artists, writers, actors, and musicians. One of their projects was writing the histories of the areas in which they lived. These have proven invaluable for today's historians. The CCC worked along the Elizabeth River and its banks to control flooding. The WPA also graded and paved local streets including "paper streets," planned streets on city maps that had never been built.

Despite the Depression, many people attempted to live as they had or as they had wanted to. Many Elizabethans had cottages at the Jersey Shore or on one of New Jersey's 500 lakes in Sussex, Warren, or Hunterdon Counties. Dances were held at the Elizabeth Country Club or the Elks Clubhouse, where a weekly dancing class was conducted by Mrs Hylick, with recitals at the Masons Mosque Clubhouse. Freddy Sleckman's Orchestra played for them regularly. Debutante balls were held for the well-to-do in Elizabeth homes or hotels or university clubs in New York City. Students at Vail-Deane or Pingry School, the two private schools in the city, planned to attend the Seven Sisters or their Ivy League counterparts, while those at Battin High School or Jefferson High School made plans to attend local colleges. Summer jobs for college students were at a premium. Men with families were working in them to support the family. Many students found work on the city playgrounds.

Hitler sent his storm troopers into Austria to preserve order and announced that Austria was united with Germany in March 1938. It was the first step in his aggressive plan to capture all of Europe.

Orson Wells's play *The War of the Worlds* was broadcast on the radio on Sunday night, October 30, 1938, as a newscaster's announcement from Griggstown, New Jersey. It frightened many people who flooded the police stations with telephone calls and hurried to the highways in their cars to escape. Playwrights were warned to avoid using the news broadcasting method when presenting plays on the radio. The incident revealed how nervous people were about the world situation.

On September 16, 1940, President Roosevelt signed the first Selective Service Training Act, which required that all men between 21 and 35 years of age register

Adrian O. Murray was director of the Elizabeth Chamber of Commerce, later the Chamber of Commerce of Eastern Union County.

for military service. This was augmented after the country went to war. Machine shops and large industries in Elizabeth began to retool to make products needed for the war in Europe. The 30-acre Bayway Terminal Corporation building on Bayway Avenue, with its ten buildings devoted to warehousing and manufacturing, became a hub of activity as several companies became active handling foods, coats, cotton products, and chemicals. The raw materials arrived at the terminal by rail and were shipped from the company's docks on the Arthur Kill by ship. The new jobs in these and other industries took America out of the Depression. The 40-hour work week became effective in October 1940. Until then many people worked 44 hours a week. Prior to 1938, the work week was 48 hours, or six days long.

On December 8, 1941, the day after the Japanese attacked Pearl Harbor, fear swept through the Elizabeth area as false rumors of an invasion by air passed from resident to resident. Although German U-boats were active along the New Jersey coast, no landings were reported and the people began to feel safer. In February, all clocks were put on Eastern Daylight Savings Time and stayed that way throughout the war. Blankets were placed along the boardwalks at the shore to shadow building lights and street and boardwalk lights were ordered to be turned off in a blackout to prevent the submarines from shelling the shore. Scrap rubber and metal drives were conducted to recycle these valuable materials for the war effort. Because of shortages, price ceilings were set on wages, the cost of goods, and rents. There was rationing on sugar, coffee, shoes, gasoline, meat, and other food. All non-essential construction was prohibited. Cloth was in short supply and women's skirts became shorter and men's double breasted suits were eliminated to save material.

Life went on despite the war. On May 30,1943, the First Baptist Church celebrated its hundredth anniversary. The church was begun June 5, 1843 and the unusual red brick sanctuary was built in 1872. The church continues to serve Elizabeth today.

Boxwood Hall was dedicated in 1943. The house was purchased by Elias Boudinot in 1772 and was his residence until 1795. While he lived in it, the house was known as the Boudinot Mansion. Boudinot called his home Boxwood Hall, because of the shrubs around it. He received news of the signing of the Treaty of Paris ending the Revolutionary War in the mansion, while he was president of the Continental Congress. He also entertained President-elect George Washington, his cabinet, and some of his officers at lunch on April 23, 1789. Boudinot sold the dwelling to Jonathan Dayton, youngest signer of the U.S. Constitution, who lived in it from 1795 until his death in 1824. It was later a private girls' school, then a boarding house, the headquarters for the Elizabeth Chapter of the American Red Cross, and the Home for Aged Women. The Boxwood Hall Memorial Association was formed in 1940 and purchased the property after the home was moved to 111 DeHart Place. The state provided the $10,000 needed for its restoration. A fourth floor that was added when it served as the Home for Aged Women was removed. The DeHart Place building became the Reverend Charles S. Hudson Center for Hope Hospice.

Elizabeth's churches, synagogues, and various social agencies planned programs for local servicemen. Many of the servicemen, however, preferred the half-hour trip to the excitement of New York City. A few of the servicemen were housed at the YMCA. Hotel space was limited as servicemen who were stationed at Newark Airport crowded every room. A former railroad building near North Broad and East Grand Streets was turned in a United Services Organization clubhouse that opened nightly for servicemen. Approved young women from the city were the hostesses and dancing partners. The nightly program featured refreshments, games, and conversations. In the summer picnics were arranged in nearby parks.

On the night of February 29, 1944, the Westminster Presbyterian Church on North Broad Street at Prince Street facing Military Square was destroyed by fire. The cause was never determined. Only the church's two towers, the pastor's study, church office, and vestibule were spared. The communion service and some of the church records stored in a closet in the larger tower were saved by Reverend Otto W. Buschgen, pastor from 1937 to 1948. He believed strongly in cordial relations with other faiths and was scheduled to speak on Sunday, February 20, 1948, at Temple B'nai Israel on "Brotherhood through the Cooperative Efforts of Protestants, Catholic and Jewish Faiths" when he suffered a fatal heart attack.

Elizabeth native Vice Admiral William F. Halsey, Allied commander in the South Pacific, was in command when his fleet smashed Japan's effort to recapture the Guadalcanal-Tulagi area in the Solomon Islands. He was honored at a enormous parade in Elizabeth at war's end.

Boxwood Hall was built c. 1749 by Mayor Samuel Woodruff. Sold to Elias Boudinot—future president of the Continental Congress—in 1772, it entertained President-elect George Washington in 1789 and the Marquis de Lafayette in 1824.

When the war ended in 1945, people in Elizabeth searched for news about their relatives in the former occupied nations of Europe. Hundreds were found and were invited to Elizabeth. They were assisted by their relatives here in finding housing, jobs, and education if they needed it. Many of them crowded courses in English as a Second Language. They merged into the ethnic population. Elizabeth residents born in European countries visited those countries to observe the damage. Most of them came back to Elizabeth happy to be in New Jersey.

The First Presbyterian Church was destroyed by fire during a wedding on June 25, 1946. The Westminster and First Presbyterian Churches considered uniting, but decided against it. The Westminster Church purchased the old Davidson mansion on North Avenue between Salem and Westminster Avenues, razed the mansion, and built a new church with ample parking. The plans were prepared by Geofrey Poggi, a popular city architect, who also prepared plans for the Elmora Branch of the Elizabeth Public Library, the chapel in the Evergreen Cemetery, and the administration building in Warinanco Park for the Union County Parks Department. The First Presbyterian Church was rebuilt inside the walls of the post-Revolutionary building.

Memories of another war were revived in December 1946, when the City of Elizabeth donated the old Revolutionary War training place, the strip of land in front of the First Presbyterian Church, to the church. The only restriction on the gift of the commons to the church was that it "be used as it has for so many years past, purely as a plaza or lawn for the beautification of the church property." The 40-foot wide commons extends from the church, along the front of its cemetery, to Caldwell Place.

The end of the war was also marked in 1946 by several strikes by telephone, steel, electrical, automobile, mine, and railroad workers all seeking higher pay. It was no longer unpatriotic to strike. Soldiers returning home sought their old jobs. Some of them held them and attended colleges and technical and business schools at night to be better trained for those jobs, while others attended college full time, all under the G.I. Bill that paid for their educations. The schools were full. It appeared as though America would have the best educated people in the world.

Women who had responded to the nation's call for workers resumed their lives as housewives, but many, having had a taste of a paycheck, continued to stay in the work place and began seeking equal pay for equal jobs in the classroom, bank, insurance office, store, or factory. They also began to seek public office. Florence P. Dwyer was elected to the General Assembly in 1949 and served from 1950 to 1956, when she was elected to Congress and served until 1972, while Mildred Barry Hughes, who resided in the Blue House at Liberty Hall, served in the General Assembly from 1958 to 1960 and the State Senate from 1972 to 1974. Women also became members of the Boards of Education, City Councils, and municipal boards, officers in banks, and department heads in businesses and stores.

Various service organizations joined to form the United Service Organization canteen near the Central Railroad off Broad Street for servicemen and women stationed in the Newark-Elizabeth area during World War II.

Frank Brennan was the wartime police chief, serving from 1936 to 1955, when he was replaced by Edward E. Flaherty, who held the post from 1956 to 1962. Brennan served as a law enforcement officer from 1913, and Flaherty from 1920. Fire chiefs during the same period were Harry Jarvais, 1943–1944; Patrick Keelan, 1944–1954; Edward F. Deignan, 1954–1963; and John Burns, 1963–1974. Mayors were James T. Kirk, 1939–1951; Nicholas S. LaCorte, 1952–1956, who was the only Republican mayor to be elected a second time in 40 years and the first Italian mayor; and Stephen J. Bercik, 1957–1965, who was a member of the Waterfront Commission of New York Harbor. Fire directors were Edward F. Deignan, 1965–1967; and George Forrester, 1967–1979.

Maurice "Lefty" McDermont, a graduate of St. Patrick's High School, played with both the New York Yankees and the Boston Red Sox. Carl Dent, who attended Jefferson High School, played with the Negro Baseball League from 1950 to 1957. He was a veteran of the U.S. Army in Japan and was employed by the New Jersey Turnpike Authority until 1989, when he retired.

During the hot summer of 1947, officials in New Jersey wrote a new state constitution, its third, in an un-airconditioned gymnasium at Rutgers University in New Brunswick. It was adopted and replaced the 1844 constitution. It provided for a strong governor limited to two four-year terms, simplified the court system, provided for four-year terms for state senators and two-year terms for assembly members, and prohibited discrimination in race, color, sex, national origin, and religion in the state's Bill of Rights.

The Port Authority of New York leased the Newark Airport and Port Newark from the City of Newark. Both airport and seaport had served the nation well during the war years. The airport accommodated thousands of planes, while the seaport was used to build and service ships as well as transporting supplies and importing products after the war. Soon both facilities extended into Elizabeth.

The sound of the hammer, drill, and bulldozer became familiar as industries built new factories or additions. Subdivisions were cut through farm land and the 118-mile-long New Jersey Turnpike was completed in 1952. The 143-mile-long Garden State Parkway was opened in 1955.

The construction of the New Jersey Turnpike ended forever the use of the Elizabeth River by ocean-going vessels. From 1664, when the area was settled, Broad Street at the stone bridge was the head of navigation. The stone bridge was a fixed bridge. The other bridges between the Arthur Kill and Broad Street were movable. Several bridges were built over the river to carry street traffic across them. Each bridge placement and replacement required adoption of state laws to permit the erection of a draw or swing bridge. The bridge had to be approved by the Essex County Board of Chosen Freeholders before 1857, and by the Union County Board after that date and the U.S. Army Corps of Engineers. After the U.S. Coast Guard was formed, it policed the river on a routine basis.

The bridges were at six locations: South Front Street, South First Street, Baltic Street, Bridge Street, South Street, and Summer Street. At first they were all draw or swing bridges. Gradually they were replaced by the bascule-type draw bridge.

Their special feature was a huge cement block counterweight that was suspended over the road bed as a counterbalance when the bridge opened.

The U.S. Corps of Engineers moved the head of navigation back from Broad Street to Trenton Avenue. The construction of the Turnpike removed Baltic Street from the map and isolated the 1916 bridge on a 4-acre site. The old bridge was sold for scrap in 1954 after efforts to sell the complete structure failed.

Meanwhile the South Street, Bridge Street, and Summer Street Bridges were designated as fixed by the Corps. Only the South Front Street and South First Street bridges remained movable, and only the South Front Street Bridge was lifted frequently enough to require a full-time bridge tender.

The South First Street Bridge had a bridge tender five days a week during daytime hours to permit barges carrying oil, trap rock, and lumber and pleasure crafts to pass through. Built in 1908, the bridge was 80 feet long and 32 feet wide. The bridge was rehabilitated in 1975 and again in 1981. In July 1984, fire destroyed the bridge tender's house with its controls. Fortunately the bridge was down at that time and it continues in that position today.

Because of the construction of the Turnpike, the decision of the Corps of Engineers, and arson, Union County has only one drawbridge, the South Front Street Bridge. The present bridge was approved in 1920 and opened in 1922. It was built by the American Bridge Company at the mouth of the Elizabeth River 1 mile northeast of the Goethals Bridge and close to Elizabeth Avenue. The Highway and Electrical Railway Bridge Company fabricated the steel. The bridge is opened an estimated 2,000 times a year. The original timber roadway was replaced in 1956 with a steel deck and the bridge was repaired in 1974. The bridge, because of its unique counterweight, is considered a historic site.

Churches that flourished in the 1920s seemed to shrink in the 1950s. Talks were held among several of the traditional denominations about merging, but the congregations objected because of ritual difference or because they felt that their site was historically important and should be preserved. St. John's Episcopal Church met with representatives of Christ, Trinity, and St. Augustine, and the First Presbyterian Church met with trustees of Second and Third. No agreements were reached. Meanwhile some churches just disappeared. The Moravian Church and the Congregational Churches closed. Records of the Moravian Church were turned over to a church in Union Township.

L. Ron Hubbard of Aberdeen Road started the Church of Scientology at his home. He attracted both Catholics and Protestants who were interested in his books on scientology and dianetics. They are a system of thought to erase individual stresses and improve communication with marriage partners, friends, and fellow workers. John Travolta, the actor, is the best known follower of this philosophy.

Dr. Elbert H. Pogue, a physician, came to Elizabeth after World War II to establish his medical practice. By 1965, he was president of the Union County Medical Society, formed in 1857. Dr. Greeley Brown practiced medicine in Elizabeth for 50 years. Dr. Richard Payne was the eighth of thirteen children of an elevator operator in Elizabeth, studied at Yale University, and received his medical degree from Harvard. He is a cancer specialist and chief of the Sloan-Kettering Hospital's department of palliative care in New York City. Edward Pierson, a Chicago native and bass baritone, appeared in Broadway shows and with the New York City Opera, while he lived in the Elmora section of the city. All are African Americans.

World War II introduced Elizabeth youths to the world and they loved it. Many of them had only been a few miles away from home before the war. Vacations in the Catskills, New Jersey's lakes, or the Jersey Shore were the norm. Few had traveled even to neighboring states such as Pennsylvania, Delaware, or Connecticut. Only the rich went to Florida or California. After the war, many of the veterans attended colleges out of state, while others decided to seek job opportunities in them. Their parents and siblings wanted to visit them, creating a traveling public in the 1950s. Various businesses awarded their salesmen with trips to Paris or Rome. The demand for better and faster roads grew as the public traveled.

The Singer Manufacturing Company retooled after the war in order to resume the manufacture of sewing machines. The company's growth was phenomenal. Workers seeking higher pay went on strike for five months in 1949. It was a rough five months for the employees, as many lost their new houses and were forced to live with relatives. By the 1950s, Singer appeared to have recovered from the strike and hired some 10,000 employees. The company said it was the largest plant in

Strikers from Local 481 picket the Singer plant from a rowboat on Newark Bay in 1949. The five-month strike was to guarantee job security for Singer employees.

127

Union County prosecutor Edward Cohn took an ax to illegal slot machines seized in Elizabeth in 1950. It was the practice at the time to destroy the machines.

the world. It began to open sewing centers throughout the world including 1,300 in the United States and Canada. It employed people to teach sewing, conduct fashion shows, and sell dress patterns. Some 61,444 persons were employed world-wide in sales of the machines. It was estimated that more than 29 million women and girls sewed and it was the chief hobby for women in America. Charles Aquilina claimed that the Japanese word for sewing machine is "Singer" because of the popularity of the machine in Japan.

New companies began to appear. One of these was the MDM Technology Co. at 333 First Street, which did direct mailing laser printing and computer processing. It was started by Louis Peck in 1951, taken over by his son-in-law Warren Grover in 1964, and sold in 1996.

After the war the Newark Airport was returned to the city in 1946. It was leased to the Port Authority by the City of Newark on March 22, 1948. Low-flying civilian flights increased. The residents of Newark's Weequahic section, Hillside, and Elizabeth, whose houses were under the flight path, complained about the low flying noisy planes on both takeoffs and landings.

Disaster from the air struck Elizabeth three times in 58 days between December 16, 1951 and February 11, 1952, when three airplanes crashed. The first crash was on a cold, sunny Sunday afternoon when 56 passengers and crew aboard a C-46 that had just taken off from Newark Airport crashed into the Elizabeth River near Westfield Avenue on its way back to the airport. The crash apparently was caused by engine trouble.

The second one, on a rainy foggy afternoon at 3:45 on January 22,1952, was a Convair 240 that went down behind Battin High School on Williamson and South Streets. Twenty-three passengers including Secretary of War Robert Patterson and seven Elizabeth residents on the ground were among the victims.

The third and last crash was at 12:21 a.m. on Monday, February 11, 1952, by an outbound airplane that hit the top of the apartments at 610 Salem Avenue, killing four persons and crashing on Westminster Avenue behind the Janet Memorial Home, the orphanage, killing 25 passengers. Unlike the two earlier crashes, a stewardess survived this one and told police that the plane began losing altitude after reaching about 1,500 feet, "The two engines gave out before we could return to the airport," she said. Thirty-four passengers also survived.

Less than three hours later the Port of New York Authority ordered the Newark Airport closed and all aircraft were diverted to fields in New York. The airport was reopened November 15, 1952, after it was determined that the port's facilities were not at fault in the crashes. The crashes were among the first uses of mutual aid in Union County, where surrounding towns were permitted to send their personnel to assist in an emergency. It also made police officials realize that fire and police and other emergency personnel needed more training to handle emergencies.

Luis Martinez became Elizabeth's first Hispanic police officer when he joined the Elizabeth Police Department on December 10, 1953, with 17 other new recruits. Unfortunately he suffered a heart attack and died at his home on November 12, 1957.

Ground was broken for the present one-story building for the Benedictine Academy in 1953. At the same time a cottage was erected for the chaplain of the convent adjacent to the Motherhouse. It now is used by the Father Hudson Hospice and is known as Theo House for terminally-ill patients. Many people assisted the Benedictine Sisters in their efforts to help the poor of Elizabeth. One of these was Harry A. Grassman, a partner with his brother, Edward J. Grassman, in an engineering firm. Edward was a former city engineer. He developed the Westminster Section in the late 1930s through the 1950s. Most of the dwellings were Georgian Colonial architecture and he demanded that they be painted white.

Captain James B. McGovern, a World War II ace pilot, was shot down over Dien Bien Phu in Vietnam in 1954, where the United States was supporting the Indo-Chinese government after the French pulled out. Captain McGovern's brother John, a reporter, was checking the Associated Press wire at *The Elizabeth Daily Journal* when word of his brother's death came over the wire. Captain McGovern's body was recovered in 2002.

On February 14, 1954, *The Elizabeth Daily Journal* celebrated its 175th anniversary at a party at the Waldorf-Astoria Hotel in New York City for the entire staff and board of directors. Governor Robert B. Meyner and other officials also were guests. The highlight of the evening was an enormous birthday cake cut by Mrs. Gwen Crane, chairman of the board and mother of Robert C. Crane, editor and publisher. It would be the last large celebration for the staff. A special anniversary edition tracing the history of the *Journal* and the area was published on February 16, 1954, the actual anniversary.

Robert C. Crane became a state senator in 1956 and served until 1962. He became acting governor for a day on January 9, 1962, when Governor Meyner left the state for lunch in Pennsylvania. Meyner gave Crane the honor because Crane was terminally ill, dying three months later on April 14, 1962.

It was fortunate that September 11, 1958, was a Jewish holiday when a train from Elizabethport to Bayonne on the Newark Bay Bridge went through an open drawbridge into Newark Bay, killing 48 people. Normally the train carried some 300 passengers to New York City where they were employed in the New York garment district. Most of them stayed home to observe the holiday that day. The disaster was never explained or understood. It became known as the George "Snuffy" Stirnweiss accident because the New York Yankee baseball player was enroute to Yankee Stadium for a game and was one of the victims. In 1945, Stirnweiss was awarded the American League batting championship. The bridge was removed shortly after the accident.

A new Elizabeth Channel at the seaport was dug in 1958. It paralleled the Newark Channel, which opened in 1962. Since then the channels have been dredged frequently. The Elizabeth Channel is at the mouth of Bound Creek, the traditional boundary between Elizabeth and Newark.

A major change in the Police Department was made on March 1, 1961, when Rolf Harbo, a former special agent with the Federal Bureau of Investigation, was named the first police director after the Board of Police Commissioners was eliminated. He served until he became ill. Police Chief William J. Mulkeen was appointed police director and police chief June 12, 1962, and served in both capacities until his death on May 27, 1964. He joined the department in 1941. Deputy Police Chief Michael Roy filled both posts until January 1, 1965, when he became police chief serving until he retired in 1981. Roy, whose name was actually Mitro Roj, also joined the force in 1941. Both served in World War II.

Following the rise of Fidel Castro in Cuba, hundreds of Cubans migrated to Elizabeth. Many of them were well-educated and were professors, teachers, doctors, poets, and lawyers in Cuba. They settled in the Port area and operated stores and restaurants along Elizabeth Avenue until they became acclimated to America. Advertising salesmen for the *Journal* used to say they saved Elizabeth Avenue. They started their own weekly newspaper *La Voz*, a Spanish-language newspaper.

In the early 1960s, Reverend Joseph J. Garlic started the Elizabethport Presbyterian Center as an inner-city mission to assist residents from pre-schoolers to seniors. Programs are conducted throughout the day. There is a day nursery at 154 First Street, a program to assist students doing their homework, and a scholarship awards program for high school seniors planning to enter college. In 1985, the center started Brand New Day Inc., a low-income housing corporation to purchase and renovate or build new housing for persons with limited incomes. The agency now is separate from the center. It renovated the old St. Joseph's

Academy, built and sold ten townhouses to first time home buyers, remodeled a building to contain the day nursery with apartments overhead, an apartment-store building, and a row of stores. Both the center and the housing corporation are supported by churches in the Elizabeth Presbytery. Brand New Day has representatives of both the Roman Catholic and Jewish community on its board of directors.

In 1962, the state directed that all orphanages be closed. The Janet Memorial Home between Westminster and Salem Avenues was one of them. Orphans henceforth were placed in foster care. St. Walburga's Orphanage was closed in 1931. A few of the older girls were housed in the Motherhouse while they attended the Academy.

Also in the early 1960s, Edward J. Grassman and Mary Alice Barney Kean formed the Elizabethtown Historical Foundation. The foundation purchased three historic houses: the Bonnell House, the oldest dwelling in Elizabethtown; The Belcher-Ogden House, home of Royal Governor Jonathan Belcher and state Governor Aaron Ogden, and the St. John's Parsonage, once owned by St. John's Episcopal Church. They restored the dwellings to their original splendor. Mrs. Kean then revived the Union County Historical Society, which met in the parsonage for many years.

The first incident of racial unrest in Elizabeth occurred in 1963, when the Union County Courthouse annex was being constructed and African Americans questioned why they were absent from the construction crews. Many of the labor unions in New Jersey were open only to men whose fathers and grandfathers had

This vertical-lift bridge over the Arthur Kill for the Baltimore and Ohio Railroad was built in 1954 to replace several earlier bridges at the same site.

belonged to the same union. This law within the unions would exclude many people, including blacks. The African Americans demonstrated at the construction site that year and again in 1964, and at an apartment complex in North Elizabeth. John Harvard, who represented them, attempted to let the press and public know how unfair this exclusion was.

On August 14, 1964, rioters in the Port broke windows and threw molotov cocktails. Mayor Steven Bercik called municipal leaders together and order was restored. Bercik was defeated in the November election by Thomas Dunn and it was generally believed that the riot contributed to Bercik's defeat. He became a Superior Court Judge.

There were some disturbances in 1965 and 1967, which resulted in the formation of the disorder platoon in the police department. The officers were trained at Fort Dix. Civil Rights activists and enforcement of laws on equal opportunity opened up many jobs for African Americans in employment. Nida Edwards Thomas, a social worker and educator, was in the forefront of efforts to provide equal opportunity for all.

Ground was broken in March 1965 for the new Benedictine Motherhouse and chapel adjacent to the Davis mansion. The new building was L-shaped. The chapel faced North Broad Street with large statues of Saint Benedict and Saint Scholastica on either side of the main entrance. The seal of Saint Benedict was above the central door. There was a bell tower. The exterior wall closest to the mansion contained a cloister passage flanked by open arches. At the rear of the

Elizabethport began handling container ships in 1958 on the Elizabeth Channel. The port was the prototype for most of the world's terminals and a pioneer in handling container cargo.

mansion was the infirmary wing with lobby, a series of parlors, bedrooms for guests and patients, suites for community officials, an office, and a large conference room. There also are a four-story residence hall, a general services building, and a four-car garage.

For a time the sisters considered a junior college on the grounds. The New Jersey Department of Education visited the nunnery and decided there were too few candidates for the college. It was recommended that they attend Seton Hall University.

After Robert Kennedy was shot in a hotel in Los Angeles and died a few hours later in June 1968, a funeral train carrying his body from Washington to Boston was scheduled to pass through the Elizabeth station on the Pennsylvania tracks. Hundreds of people crowded along the station platform and along the tracks beside it. As the train approached some of the people pressed forward onto the express tracks and were struck by a passing express train. Two were killed and three others injured.

The quiet of the night was disturbed on December 5, 1970, when there was a loud explosion followed by the breaking of glass and ringing of burglar alarms in area stores. Fires in several storage tanks at the Exxon Refinery were the cause of the explosion. The shock waves from the explosion caused store windows to be broken 7 miles away, while some closer to the refinery were undamaged. The broken windows gave looters an opportunity to steal products from the stores as local fire departments attempted to secure the properties until replacement windows could be installed in the morning.

The Vietnam Conflict became the most unpopular military action the nation ever fought. Hundreds of anti-war demonstrations were held. Young people from Elizabeth participated in bus trips to Washington to march with others in protest of the conflict. Hundreds of young men fled to Canada or got married young and fathered children to avoid the draft. The Democratic Presidential Convention in Chicago opened on August 26, 1968, with hundreds of demonstrators against the conflict in the streets. The election of Richard Nixon as President over Hubert Humphrey was because of the Vietnam Conflict, political analysts said.

The public in general treated the young service personnel with contempt. Those who returned home were called murderers. One veteran who lost his arm in battle was told, "It serves you right." Unlike their fathers and mothers after World War II, there were no "Welcome Home" signs, no parades, no ceremonies for those who survived. Nationwide some 58,229 men and women were killed.

In Elizabeth, schools for the gifted and talented were established and all children who qualified attended them. In the adjacent communities of Union Township and Hillside, the state charged the communities with de facto segregation. The children in the elementary schools were bused to achieve racial desegregation. The state forced the change when educators realized that separate and equal education in the schools of the state failed to exist. Hillside's population next to the Weequahic section of Newark turned from Jewish to African American in 1967, followed Weequahic's example. Union's Vauxhall Section became African

American in the early 1900s. The Jefferson School there became Central Six for all sixth graders (now Central Five for all fifth graders) in the township. The middle schools and the high school were mixed. Busing was protested by many homeowners in Hillside and other communities because there was no busing in the communities and many residents purchased homes close to the schools so that the children would be close to home. They were ignored. The day of the neighborhood school had ended.

The population of Elizabeth dropped to 109,912 in 1940. It rose to 112,817 in 1950, but dropped again to 107,698 in 1960. In 1970 it went up to 112,654, and down to 106,101 in 1980. The census listed 110,002 persons in 1990. By 2000, the population was tabulated at 120,568, the highest figure in the city's history. Officials throughout the state believe that the census figures are low. The population was nearly 60 percent Hispanic, 20 percent white, and 20 percent African American. They fear that many people, especially the new immigrants, go uncounted. The number of undocumented aliens is unknown.

Elizabeth police officers underwent riot training after the nationwide riots in 1967. The training was never put to use.

7. CHANGES 1968–2003

The years following the civil disturbances of the 1960s were full of changes in Elizabeth as people attempted to cope with the introduction of new technology, higher costs of living, and changes in ethnic and religious diversity.

Mayor Thomas G. Dunn, who held the position of mayor longer than anyone else in the city's history, served from 1965 to 1991 He also was a state senator from 1974 to 1978. He kept the peace in the 1960s when adjacent Newark and nearby Plainfield were erupting in racial violence. He enraged the police and fire departments in 1968 when he suggested the two departments be merged to save money and increase efficiency. The recommendation died quickly.

Mayor Dunn was known for being a maverick. He refused to follow the Democratic Party line if he disagreed with an action. He frequently supported the Republican Party's actions or those of Independents. His independence was praised by many and of course criticized by others. Dunn implemented the Elizabeth River Flood Control Plan, which put the river into a walled viaduct in 1979. The Trotter's Lane Branch of the river was encased in a storm sewer in the early 2000s, which also helped to eliminate flooding in Elizabeth at the Union Township line on Morris Avenue. Dunn also supervised the planting of flowering trees along the streets in the center of Elizabeth returning the city to its well-known tree-lined status.

The new Elizabeth High School with the Thomas G. Dunn Sr. Sports Center opened in 1977. The sports center is constructed so that it may be closed off from the rest of the school for basketball games, concerts, and other events. The first ethnic festival in Elizabeth, for instance, was conducted from June 26–28, 1979, at the Sports Center. The school is on the property once used by Peter Breidt City Brewing Company at 900 Pearl Street. A parcel of land opposite the brewery between the street and the Elizabeth River, once occupied by small workingmen's homes, became the parking lot for the high school.

The disappearance of Protestants from the city forced the unification of some churches. Siloam Presbyterian united with Hope Presbyterian because the members of both congregation had decreased significantly. Reverend Hawkins, the African-American pastor, served as pastor of the united African-American church with the white congregation until his death. In 1972, the Madison Avenue Presbyterian Church united with its founder, the Westminster Presbyterian Church, and in 1984 the Third Presbyterian Church next to City Hall joined them, making the church the Third Westminster Presbyterian Church. Reverend Dr. Robert W. Scott, pastor of the Westminster Church; and Reverend Dr. Guy E. Lambert Jr., pastor of the Third Church, became co-pastors of the Third Westminster Presbyterian Church. Both ministers retired at the same time. Reverend Thomas Hall was called as pastor in 1990 and died in his church office in November 1997. Reverend Calvin Hsu became pastor in 2001. The church is noted for its diverse congregation including Africans, African-Americans, Indians, Filipinos, and other Americans with varied ethnic backgrounds. The children's program includes a highly acclaimed Music Institute.

St. Augustine's Episcopal Church, an African-American congregation, joined Christ Episcopal Church in 1973. The combined church changed its name to the Church of the Resurrection. The 135-year-old Christ Church building was destroyed by fire on January 16, 1987. The sanctuary, rectory, and parish hall were considered too badly damaged to restore. It was decided to merge the Church of the Resurrection with the Trinity Episcopal Church on North Broad Street at Chestnut Street in 1988. The all-white Trinity sanctuary went through an extensive building renovation before the mostly black Church of the Resurrection

Mayor Thomas G. Dunn watched construction of a flood control project on the Elizabeth River near Pearl Street in 1979. The river was walled in to prevent it overflowing onto city streets at high tide or during heavy rain storms.

joined it. The formal merger was on March 20, 1991. The combined church became the St. Elizabeth Episcopal Church in recognition of the City of Elizabeth, where it is located, and as a tribute to several saintly women in history, according to Reverend Charles Brown, then rector of the church. Richard Upjohn, the well-known architect, designed the church building erected in 1871. It is in the Gothic style and looks much like an English country church.

Elizabeth's Koreans formed the Korean Presbyterian Church at the Westminster Presbyterian Church in 1975. Within two years, the congregation was able to purchase the former recreation center of the New Jersey Standard Oil Company built prior to World War I at 700–714 Bayway Avenue. The Abby Rockefeller Cottage is used by the custodian who lives on the grounds. The program offers worship services, English as a second language, karate, Korean dancing, history and language for children, and Americanization classes for adults.

Mayor Dunn also supported the strikers at *The Daily Journal*, the city's only daily newspaper, when they went on strike on April 18, 1979, in an effort to save the jobs of the editorial, advertising, and circulation staffs. The strike was called after a series of across the board layoffs caused partially by new technology. Mayor Dunn assisted the New York Local of The Newspaper Guild in starting *The Community Paper*, a union-operated, five days a week tabloid. *The Community Paper*, while considered good, never caught on in circulation. The Guild pulled out its support of the paper in January 1980, and the Hagadone Newspaper Inc., the *Journal*'s new owners as of July 1975, provided some severance pay to the employees due under the Guild contract. One hundred jobs were lost. The *Journal* continued to be operated by non-union personnel.

The paper was sold in 1986 to the North Jersey Newspapers Company, whose owners included W. Dean Singleton and Richard B. Scudder, the former publisher of the defunct *Newark Evening News*. The circulation declined to 30,000 a day, less than half what it had been in the 1970s when it was owned by Atlantic Newspapers Inc., headed by Ralph Ingersoll, who was backed by the Goodson-Todman TV game-show entrepreneurs.

In 1977, the *Journal* moved into a new one-story facility adjacent to the 1924 building on North Broad Street said to cost $2 million dollars. The morgue (the newspaper's library of clippings and photographs) was thrown in a dumpster during the move. These included old photographic glass plates and historic photographs of the Elizabeth area. The clippings dealt with people and subjects in the area. Computers replaced typewriters. Syndicated columns, purchased features, Associated Press and various press service stories filled up the newspaper. Local news nearly disappeared. The editorial staff dropped to six reporters. In the late 1960s, by contrast, the editorial staff had more than 50 persons. The newspaper closed on January 31, 1992, after 212 years of servicing the public. Elizabeth and Union County now lack a local daily newspaper.

Two well-known New Jersey artists are natives of Elizabeth: Maxwell Stewart Simpson and Harry Devlin. Simpson was known chiefly for his paintings depicting area history, while Devlin, once a political cartoonist, favored children's stories and architectural paintings of various styles of houses in New Jersey. He co-authored and illustrated more than 20 children's books with his wife Wende, including *The Old Black Witch* and *How Fletcher Was Hatched*. He wrote several books about architecture including *To Grandfather's House We Go: A Tour of American Homes*, *What Kind of a House is That?*, and *Portraits of American Architecture: Monuments to a Romantic Mood*.

Stephanie E. Pogue, daughter of Dr. and Mrs. Elbert H. Pogue, was chairman of the Fisk University and University of Maryland art departments and won numerous art awards and fellowships in print making, graphic arts, and drawing. She earned study and travel fellowships to India, Pakistan, and Poland. Her work is featured in several collections.

Judy Sussman, an Elizabeth native, became Judy Blume, the author of novels for girls. Most of them deal with current day problems. She also has written some adult novels.

Mary Rabadeau, one of the first five women appointed to the police department in 1978, was a police captain when she was named police director by Mayor J. Christian Bollwage in 1993. She was the first woman to hold a director's post in the state. Rabadeau later stepped down to deputy chief. She resigned in October 1995 to become chief of the transit police. Nerida Rey became Elizabeth's first Hispanic female police officer in 1986. In September 1991, the Hispanic Law Enforcement Association was organized. There were about 50 Hispanic police officers in Union County at the time. Patrolman Juan Colon was appointed president, while Sergeant John Vazquez was vice-president. The next year Vazquez was promoted to captain. Patrolman Manuel Perez Jr. became president of the association in 1992.

Meanwhile Louchaun Holmes became the first African-American female police officer. She was included in a group of officers hired in 1991 as replacement for officers who failed to return to the department after being laid off in 1989 in an economic reduction of staff. Basil Leach became the first African American to be promoted to sergeant on the Elizabeth force in 1961. He was a captain when he retired.

Since the Elizabeth Police Department was formed in 1858, seven police officers have died in the line of duty. Patrolman Robert J. Paton was shot by the occupants of a car believed to be stolen on Elizabeth Avenue at Jefferson Avenue in 1918. Police Captain John Hiney also died in 1918 when the car he was in enroute to a fire at the Bayway Chemical Company hit an iron trolley pole on South Broad and Summer Streets. He was taken to the Elizabeth General Hospital, where he died of pneumonia. Detective Michael Norton died of peritonitis while having emergency surgery at Alexian Brothers Hospital after he was kicked in the stomach by a prisoner in the magistrate court in 1922.

Patrolman John McGann was shot on West Grand Street as he was placing two prisoners arrested in a speakeasy into a taxi to be transported to Police Headquarters. The murderer, the proprietor of the speakeasy, was captured in California and returned to Elizabeth by plane. He was tried and executed. Patrolman Frank Carine was shot when he answered a call concerning a man who was behaving strangely. Several other officers also suffered gunshot wounds before the man was subdued. He was found insane and committed to the Graystone State Mental Hospital.

Patrolman William J. Kroeschel, who was riding on an ambulance running board because the vehicle was crowded, was killed in a collision with another ambulance enroute to help a young woman who had a seizure. Motorcycle Officer George N. Guempel was enroute to Springfield Township on Morris Avenue in Union to question a suspect when he was struck by another vehicle and thrown 50 feet in the air in 1941.

A plaque honoring them was placed in front of the Morrell Street headquarters in 1966, and after the new building was constructed in 1977, a tiny memorial area was dedicated on East Grand Street. The new building, costing $15 million dollars supplied by the Port Authority of New York and New Jersey through a 47-year financial agreement, has facilities for the municipal court, garage, electrical bureau, offices, detective bureau, traffic bureau, communications, ambulance services, 16 cells, indoor pistol range, a drive-up window to pay fines, and an Olympic-style gymnasium.

The department presently has 365 persons. Only one member, however, Police Lieutenant John Brennan, is the third generation of his family to serve in the department. His father John became chief and police director and his uncles Joseph Brennan, police director; and Thomas Brennan, police captain; his grandfather, Patrolman Thomas M. Brennan Sr., director of the Elizabeth Junior Police Safety Patrol. Brennan's brother Kevin is a Port Authority police officer.

Joseph Brennan, police director from 1973 to 1993, held a press conference to seek the assistance of the public in solving a homicide. He was one of four Brennans to serve with the Elizabeth Police Department.

More than 40 families presently have multiple members serving on the force at the same time. In several instances they are brothers and sisters or husbands and wives.

Many of the officers have studied at Kean College, now University, in Union. The new officers attend the Union County Police Academy at Scotch Plains. Although the trailers used as sub-stations are still in place, they are seldom used. The department had a canine corps in 1973, and one of its dogs, Champ, was the first K-9 corps dog to be killed in New Jersey while on duty in a freak accident at the Union County Jail while searching for a suspect. He was buried at the Dowd Avenue Pistol Range. The department now depends upon the K-9 corps operated by the Union County Sheriff's Office.

On April 15, 1989, 67 police officers, 53 firemen, and 81 other municipal employees were laid off, while 34 others from the two departments were demoted because the promised "distressed cities" money from the state failed to arrive. By August 1, 1989, all firemen and 51 police officers and nearly 24 municipal employees were reinstated. The layoffs caused the police, firemen, and municipal employees to unite in 1991 to elect J. Christopher Bollwage mayor instead of the long-popular Mayor Dunn, according to *The History of the Elizabeth Police Department (1858–1996)* by a committee of police officers and Chief Lester Sargent of the Union County Sheriff's Office, a local historian. The committee included John Brennan, Ronald Gamba, Richard Garry, James Ponto, Daniel

Union County Sheriff Ralph Froelich displays two of his department's K-9 dogs. Froelich was a member of the Elizabeth Police Department from 1958 to 1977 before he was elected sheriff.

Shannon, John Deresz, and Juan Guzman Jr. Sargent's father, also Lester Sargent, was a member of the department.

Since its formation, the Elizabeth Police Department has had 16 chiefs and 8 police directors. Past police chiefs are Walter S. Miller, 1858–1861; John M. Morris, 1861–1864; John Keron, 1865–1879; Johnson J. Yates, 1879–1882; William D. Jenkins, 1882–1888; Henry Austin, 1888–1892; George C. Tenney, 1892–1913; John A. Peters, January to December 1913; Michael J. Mulcahy, 1913–1935; Frank Brennan, 1936–1955; Edward Flaherty, 1956–1962; William J. Mulkeen, 1962–1965; Michael Roy, 1964–1981; John F. Brennan, 1982–1990; and Gene Mirabella, 1990–1999. John Simon, a deputy police chief, became chief on February 1, 1999. Police directors included William J. Mulkeen, 1962–1964; Gustave Brugger, 1965–1968; John F. Brennan, 1968–1969; Thomas Byrnes, 1969–1973; Joseph Brennan, 1973–1993; Mary F. Rabadeau, 1993–1995; Patrick Maloney, a retired deputy chief, 1994–1997; and James Cosgrove, a former deputy chief in the Newark Police Department, since 1998.

Elizabeth was served by eight firehouses, five engine companies, and two truck companies in the early 1970s. In January 1980, the department was reduced to seven firehouses with the closing of the old Red Jacket Engine Company 4 at 147 Elizabeth Avenue, founded as a volunteer company on March 17, 1866. Fire Engine Company 7 will close on Prince Street when work begins on the new fire headquarters on the site. The present headquarters building will be razed for a parking lot for employees. Fire Engine Company 7 building was erected in 1911, and the company was formed in 1912. The headquarters building originally was the pumphouse for the Joint Sewer Commission.

Engine Company 1, the oldest in the city, continues to be beside the Elizabeth River at the site of the Stone Bridge at 24 South Broad Street. All the other companies have been moved since their formation: Engine 2, formerly Rolla Engine 1 founded on September 3, 1852 at 1201 East Grand Street, is at 665 South Broad Street; and Engine 3, formerly volunteer company Washington Engine 3 founded in 1841 at 8 Center Street is located at 733 New Point Road.

Hibernia Engine Company 5, a volunteer company founded March 17, 1866 on Wall Street, now Magnolia Avenue, is located at 147 Elizabeth Avenue, the former location of Red Jacket Engine 4, while Jefferson Engine Company 6, founded October 1868 at 1089 Magnolia Avenue, now is at 601 Pennsylvania Avenue.

The two truck companies, originally known as Lafayette Hook & Ladder Company 1, founded May 1, 1837; and Jackson Hook & Ladder Company 1, founded June 21, 1868, are at 601 Pennsylvania Avenue and 147 Elizabeth Avenue respectively.

A wall of remembrance for those firemen who responded to their last alarms was placed in front of the Union County Court House near the Volunteer Fireman statue containing photographs and names of 16 firemen who died on duty. They included Firefighter Paul Zellner of Truck 3 on June 16, 1916; Captain William Riley of Engine 1, December 6, 1926; Firefighter William Uhlig, Truck 1, June 16, 1933; Firefighter Edward McMeek, Engine 4, October 18, 1933; Firefighter Charles Moore, Engine 1, February 9, 1934; Lieutenant Frank

Johnson, Engine 6, November 19, 1937; Lieutenant Charles Koeler, Engine 8, March 6, 1938; Firefighter Stephen Grzesiak, Engine 7, May 25, 1952; Firefighter Frank Tesnar, Engine Company 2, March 11, 1953; Firefighter Patrick Carroll, Truck 2, January 25, 1954; Firefighter James Ford, Engine 9, September 15, 1961; Deputy Chief John Higgins, December 10, 1966; Captain Philip Clark, Engine 4, January 3, 1969; Captain Joseph McNamara, Engine 9, December 9, 1969; Captain Alfred Dziedzic, Engine 4, September 23, 1972; and Captain Kenneth Feeney, Engine 6, March 20, 1980.

Fire chiefs since 1970 include John Burns, 1963–1974; Charles Malone, 1974–1977; Edward Sisk, 1977–1982; Charles Swody, 1982-1986; William Neafsey, 1896–1895; Frank LeStata, 1996–1999 Louis Kelly, 1999–present. Fire directors in the same period were George Forrester, 1967-1979; Joseph B. Sullivan, 1979-1987; John Flanagan, 1987–1992; and Edward Sisk, 1993–1998. Michael Donlin became director in 1999.

January 1, 2002 marked the 100th anniversary of the paid Elizabeth Fire Department in Elizabeth. The major celebration on September 7 featured a parade from Broad Street to the Arthur Kill, ceremonies to honor the New York Police and Firemen and the Port of New York and New Jersey Police killed in the attack on the World Trade Center on September 11, 2001. Representatives from the three departments were among the guests. The Elizabeth Fire Department sent a total of 169 of its 263 members to Ground Zero in shifts to assist in the recovery effort. The Union County Sheriff's Office sent six members of the canine unit and four dogs, who searched in the rubble for the living. Only a housecat from one of the damaged apartments was found alive three weeks after the attack.

Six residents were killed in the attack on the World Trade Center. The city erected a memorial designed by Darrio Scholis. Scholis won a contest conducted by the City Council for the best design for the memorial. It stands near the pedestrian plaza on West Grand Street at the New Jersey Transit Railroad Station. The granite monument is 8 by 6 feet in size. It shows a clock at the time the first tower was hit, the American flag in the background supporting the two towers, and the date 9/11/2001. The names of the victims are on the two towers. They were Colleen Fraser, Anthony Tempesta, Arcelia Castillo, Margaret Lewis, Carlos Da Costa, and Frankie Serrano. Three lights illuminate the monument: two for the towers and one for the date and time.

In October 2002, Donald Peterson became the first African American in the Fire Department to become a battalion chief. At the same ceremony Battalion Chiefs David Lechner and Edward Sisk were promoted to deputy chiefs, Firefighters Jorge Chavez and Joseph Hoy to captains, and Fire Captain Lathey Wirkus to battalion chief. Police Detective James "Todd" Mooney was promoted to detective sergeant in the police department and his brother Charles "Richard" Mooney to fire captain.

The Elizabeth Playhouse opened in 1994 as a non-profit theater started by Marlow and Karon Semones Ferguson in the former Third Presbyterian Church on Scott Place. The couple purchased the defunct church in 1991 and built apartments in the old school section. The rents help to support the theater along with program advertising, donations, and tickets ranging from $5 to $8. About five plays are presented each year on weekends.

Vintage prize-winning Broadway shows such as *Holiday*, *Of Mice or Men*, *Abe Lincoln in Illinois*, *No Time for Comedy*, and *Awake and Sing* are featured. The casts are composed of young actors seeking experience, lawyers, teachers, and other professionals who enjoy the theater, and professional actors. Mrs. Ferguson also has written adaptations of several plays as well as textbooks and a young adult novel *Cricket Call*. She has charge of costumes.

Reverend David R. King, rector of St. John's Episcopal Church, played a game of tennis in 1987. After he returned to his office in the church, he suffered a fatal heart attack. He had served the church since 1966. The restored chapel in the Evergreen Cemetery was named in his honor. He was a member of the cemetery's board of trustees.

Reverend James Reisner became pastor of the First Presbyterian Church in 1987. He found homeless men sleeping in the graveyard and men suffering from AIDS, as well as Hispanic Presbyterians without a church. He established an AIDS ministry on Friday nights for the victims of that disease, sought to find shelter for the homeless in the graveyard, and established a Spanish-speaking congregation in the auxiliary building. He also began Wednesday Noon worship services followed by a lunch for the general public as well as the poor. He left the

Ralph Demmy, 95, salutes the colors as they pass him in the 1973 Memorial Day parade. Demmy was the last surviving Spanish-American War veteran.

Mayor Thomas G. Dunn presented a plaque to S.J. Murphy, vice president of the Singer Manufacturing Company, on the 100th anniversary of the company in 1973.

church in the summer of 2002 to become pastor of the Westminster Presbyterian Church in Albany, New York.

Reverend Dr. Joseph R. Parrish Jr., who holds two doctorates including one in medicine, followed the Reverend Dr. King as rector in 1988. He became interested in the Habitat for Humanity program. The group built a house on Catherine Street.

The Diocese of Newark directed that Sacred Heart Roman Catholic Church close and a new Portuguese church, Our Lady of Fatima Roman Catholic Church, occupy the sanctuary at 403 Spring Street. The Portuguese congregation moved into the church in 1983. The church does not operate the school.

Decreases in church attendance were caused by death and retirements to Florida, the New England states, New Mexico, Arizona, and New Jersey's many retirement communities. In other instances young people have followed the Garden State Parkway or the New Jersey Turnpike to other counties where the house lots are larger and cheaper. In some cases people have moved into their summer homes at the Jersey Shore or on one of New Jersey's 500 lakes in the northwestern section of the state. Highways such as Routes 78 and 80 reduced travel time to city jobs and it was cheaper to winterize the dwellings than purchase new houses. Some Elizabethans have moved to communities along both sides of the Delaware River between Trenton and Port Jervis, New York for lower cost of living, more land, and easier access to the New Jersey cities.

For nine days in April 1997, St. Adalbert's Roman Catholic Church, the oldest Polish church in Union County, observed the 1,000th anniversary of the death of Wojciech Adalbert, a martyr who is considered to be the father of Catholicism in Poland. St. Wojciech, as he is called in Poland, was speared to death in the year 997. He was canonized two years after his death. The church had more than 7,000 congregants in the 1950s. It became Cuban in the 1970s and other Hispanic groups from Latin America and the Caribbean followed in the 1980s and 1990s. The church, restored shortly before the celebrations, was threatened by fire the day before the celebration began. A stained-glass window was damaged. Hundreds of former parishioners from the suburbs returned for the observance. The church was rededicated on April 23–26, 1998. The Council of Churches listed 83 churches when the census was taken for 2000. Church leaders and city officials believe that there are more because many of them are in storefronts.

The roof literally fell in at the St. Benedictine Motherhouse. Fortunately it occurred after all the nuns and the chaplain left the chapel following the morning Mass. Nobody was injured, but the long row of arches and the chapel disappeared into a pile of rubble. Only the two statues and a column were spared. They continue to face North Broad Street. A smaller replacement chapel was erected.

Social agencies eliminated some traditional services so they could concentrate on serving the community better with fewer services and eliminate duplication. The YWCA ceased being an organization featuring activities for business or professional girls and women and instead now cares for abused women and children, offering safe sanctuary to women throughout the county. The Y also seeks to end domestic violence through numerous programs including one for teenage girls and their boyfriends.

The YMCA of Eastern Union County eliminated its swimming pool so the building could be remodeled to house women and children who were homeless. Each individual woman has to keep her unit clean, prepare meals for herself and her children, and attend classes or go to work while the children are either in school or a day care facility.

The Family and Children's Society at 40 North Avenue, begun in 1893 when two agencies combined to assist abused children, continues to do so today. The society provides counseling and support services for children and their parents, assists in foster care, and attempts to solve the multiple problems of family in the twenty-first century. It seeks adoption in approved homes for some children and foster care for others. It also supplies support services and therapy to children and parents. It conducts psychiatric evaluations and psychological testing and provides parent education and conducts mental health programs. It features outreach programs at 158 First Street, Elizabeth, and 935 Park Avenue in Plainfield. It continues to be an independent private non-profit organization and it acts as a lobbying group on mental health public policy issues.

Sister Jacinta Fernandes, a former teacher, realized that much of her work was social work, not teaching. She opened St. Joseph's Service Center at 118 Division Street in a former Slovak Roman Catholic Church, which moved to Linden, to help people find a brighter future. The center serves the homeless and the materially poor. It was begun in 1983 to provide basic needs such as food, clothing, and shelter as well as services and programs that will help the individual gain the social support he or she needs to live with integrity. Working with the center is the Elizabeth Coalition to House the Homeless, a league of churches and social service agencies. The coalition assists in the homeless obtaining emergency housing and works with them until they find permanent housing.

The old bowling alley at the Second Presbyterian Church burned while workers where repairing the roof of the 1820–1821 church. Firemen who responded quickly were able to save the rest of the church from being destroyed. An addition added to the church contains a new gymnasium and classrooms for an extensive after school tutorial and recreation program. The Central Presbyterian Church in Summit also assists in tutoring children. In 2001, the church also began a Portuguese language church mostly for Brazilians in the area. Reverend John Faustini, a Presbyterian minister and the church organist, is the pastor.

The Eastern Union County YMHA-YWHA on the Union-Elizabeth line has a wide variety of programs for children through senior citizens. One does not have to be Jewish to participate. For several seasons for instance, the Elmora Presbyterian Church nearby used the Y's swimming pool for its summer Peace Camp.

Raul E. Comesanas, a Cuban-American, helped to solve a problem among two of Elizabeth's Cubans. Comesanas was commissioner of human rights for the city and published a Spanish-language newspaper in addition to teaching at Montclair State College.

146

The Elizabethport Presbyterian Center also assumed operation of a program in Plainfield Grant Avenue Community Center in 2000, to care for pre-school and schoolchildren, adults, and senior citizens.

There are numerous agencies feeding the homeless and the poor. In addition to St. Joseph's, the Elmora Presbyterian Church with assistance from other churches in Elizabeth prepares a meal each Sunday afternoon at the First Baptist Church of Cranford-Elizabeth at 402 Union Avenue. The Salvation Army in the auxiliary building of the former Temple Israel on Spring Street and East Jersey Street serves meals daily and provides shelter for the homeless. The First Presbyterian Church offers a religious service and lunch each Wednesday on Broad Street. St. John's Episcopal Church began distributing food to the needy in 1989, at reduced prices. In addition the church members deliver food to people who are unable to visit the church. The church also serves hot meals after services on Thursdays and Sundays. The YMCA provides Thanksgiving and Christmas dinners for its residents and others who would lack a place to eat on those holidays because of lack of facilities or funds.

In 1996, Iglesia en Elizabeth (Church in Elizabeth), one of the city's newest churches on U.S. Routes 1 and 9, East Grand Street, and Praise the Lord Plaza was erected. It features an underground parking area for its congregation and also provides two buses to pick up carless members. A playground for children is along the Praise the Lord Plaza adjacent to the church.

The Compamiento de Sehova Iglesia Cristiao on Newark Avenue started as a house of worship in a one-story office building. In 2000–2001, a second floor addition was added to the new sanctuary. The New Hope Memorial Baptist Church, once a small frame building on Division Street, after years of clothing sales, became a magnificent new white building.

In the 1990s, sports halls of fame were started by the Elizabeth High School and St. Patrick's Parochial High School. The inductees included both dead and living athletes as well as coaches and others who encouraged them.

Sports have been one of the main activities of many of the city's young men and women. Thomas Jefferson High School, a boys-only institution from 1945 to 1977, won the 1955 Greater Newark News Baseball Tournament five times. Joseph Kania was coach in 1954, and Frank J. Cicarell coach in 1963, 1968, and 1970. The basketball team earned the Group IV championship in 1945, and the Union County Championship eight times in 1948 and 1949 with Robert Cox as coach; in 1950, 1954, and 1955 with William Tranavitch as coach; and 1969, 1970, and 1972 with Ron Kelly as coach.

From 1982 to 2001, Elizabeth High School has been baseball section champions ten times, Watchung Conference champions eleven times, Union County Tournament champions four times, North Jersey Group IV Champions seven times, and Group IV State champions three times.

In the same time period the school has won both football sectional championships and Watchung Conference championships seven times each. Wrestling championships include two in the Watchung Conference and one in the

District XI. Boys basketball has given the school a total of 34 more championships: State Group IV, five; State Sectional championships, eight; Union County Tournament championships, ten; and Watchung Conference Championships, eleven.

The Thomas A. Edison Vocational High School, later called the Edison Technical High School, also had athletic teams from 1929 until 1977, when it became part of Elizabeth High School. George Bitton was the first athletic director, serving for ten years as basketball coach. Dan Fleischer coached from 1940 to 1947 and had a perfect season in 1946 with 16 victories, but lost in the county tournament. Under Michael Ziobro's coaching in 1948, the team won the state finals. Gene York became coach in 1954 and coached the team for 26 years, winning three vocational technical league championships. One of his players, Bruce Burnett, became captain of the Temple University basketball team and was selected for the Elizabeth Hall of Fame. York's teams had five straight winning seasons up to his final year, 1978–1979. Ken Exeleben became coach in 1979–1980 and had five winning seasons. In 1981–1982, the team won 19 games and lost 2, the first in the county and the other in the state tournaments.

Abner West devoted more than 40 years of his life to Thomas Jefferson High School, the all boys' school, as coach of football, basketball, and baseball, teacher, athletic director, and principal. He also served as director of personnel for the Elizabeth Board of Education. West led the school to championships in 1945 in Central Jersey Group IV in both basketball and football and in 1955 in the Greater Newark Baseball Tournament.

Firemen inspected unmarked drums at the Chemical Control Corporation after an explosion and fire in 1980. It was revealed that CCC was illegally dumping chemicals in the river.

148

In addition to sports in the high schools, the YMCA and the YMHA-YWHA sponsor numerous bowling, baseball, and basketball leagues. The YMCA also sponsored industrial and church leagues. The church bowling league started by the YMCA was the last to function, ending in 1997. The Little League and the American Legion League flourish.

When the prosperous and productive factories of the nineteenth and twentieth centuries moved or closed, they left Elizabeth with an undesirable gift—brownfields—caused by the dumping of various chemicals on the ground, in the Elizabeth River, or in the aquifer tainting them all. The hazards went unrecognized until the middle of the twentieth century when various remedial cures were considered and implemented. For some parcels it was too late but for others there were cures. Some 200 brownfields are listed in the Elizabeth area. Some of them have been capped and probably will never be used because so many chemicals have entered the soil.

The site of the former Chemical Control Corporation (CCC) on the Elizabeth River and South Front Street is considered the worse brownfield in the city. The company picked up toxic chemicals from area factories and was supposed to dispose of them legally. The hazard was discovered one rainy night in 1979, after one of the owners was observed on Doremus Avenue in Newark dumping a 55-gallon tank of unknown chemicals on the street. When CCC was inspected, officials found gallons of unknown chemicals in drums on the property and a pipe leading to the river where the chemicals could wash up and down the Elizabeth River with the tide. On the night of April 21, 1980, there was a tremendous explosion followed by a fire.

Hundreds of the drums erupted, throwing chemicals and pieces of metal into the air. The cause of the fire was never determined. The owners were tried, convicted, and sent to federal prison and the state attempted to clean up the four-and-a-half acre property. Numerous residents in the area complained in later years that their health problems started with the fire. The debris was removed and the property fenced, but city and state officials continue to believe the plot is a hazard to the health of people who might use it.

The most outstanding achievement of brownfield elimination is the construction of Jersey Gardens, the largest shopping mall in New Jersey. Built on a former dump, it opened on October 21, 1999. Facilities include a 20-screen multiplex theater, a food court and four restaurants, coat and package checking, lockers, and a multilingual translation system. Foreign currency may be exchanged. Free entertainment is provided in the central court. A Jeepers! America's indoor theme park and a children's play area are available.

New highways carry traffic from Exit 13A on the New Jersey Turnpike to the mall. Also within an easy distance are Routes 1–9, 21, 22, 78, and the Garden State Parkway. The Goethals Bridge to Staten Island is south of the mall. The mall is served by public transportation including New Jersey Transit bus routes 24, 40, and 111. There is daily bus service from the Port Authority Bus Terminal in midtown Manhattan to the mall and there is a free shuttle daily from the Newark Liberty International Airport at Monorail Station E to the mall.

When the funding is approved, a light rail system will stop at the Jersey Gardens. The rail will connect the Elizabeth Railroad Station near Broad Street with the Newark Liberty International Airport and the Newark Pennsylvania Station. Known as Air Train Newark, the existing airport monorail serves a new monorail station off Haynes Avenue in Newark that opened in October 2001. It connects the airport with the former Pennsylvania Railroad tracks and the stations in Newark and New York. The station lacks parking lots because it is for rail passengers only. It is hoped that the light rail system will connect the airport with Plainfield via the old Central Railroad right of way.

Efforts are being made to reactivate the New Jersey portion of the old Staten Island Rapid Transit Railroad between Cranford and Staten Island. Plans are being made to refurbish it for freight trains only. The tracks extend from the New Jersey Transit tracks in Cranford to Roselle, Linden, and Elizabeth across the Arthur Kill on the lift bridge. When revived it will be known as the Union County Central Railroad. Eventually the plans would carry trains using it to New York City. Residents who purchased homes near the abandoned tracks object to the revival of rail service and action is stalled.

Private and public funds are being used to rebuild the city. Marine Village, a 35-unit townhouse complex costing $5 million, was built in 2002 by Brand New Day Inc., the Elizabeth Housing Authority, and RPM Development Group of Montclair. It overlooks the Arthur Kill. The townhouses feature landscaped grounds, balconies, and two or three bedrooms. The units are for people who earn too much money to qualify for public housing but too little to buy a house or rent market-rate apartments.

Private developers have built about 150 two-family homes in the Port area in the past two years. Some of the new dwellings are being sold for as much as $200,000. This is the same amount charged for houses uptown or in the suburbs.

Two apartment complexes built by the city containing 655 apartment units for persons with low incomes are gradually being demolished and replaced by single family houses. They are Pioneer Homes built in 1941 and Migliore Manor built in 1960. Mravlag Manor at 688 Maple Avenue, the third family housing complex with three buildings and 423 units built in 1940, has been renovated. The housing authority was created in 1939, to provide safe, decent, and affordable housing. It houses 3,500 persons.

Replacing Pioneer Homes are 169 semi-detached townhouses known as Portside II. These units must be reserved for low-income households from 30 to 45 years. Seventy-two rental townhouse units called Portside Commons are on the Migliore Manor site. Eventually all the buildings at both Pioneer Homes and Migliore Manor will be replaced by single units. They are being financed by state and federal government funds and the federal HOPE VI grant to the Elizabeth Housing Authority. The city hopes that 600 townhouses will be completed by 2004.

Empty lots are fast disappearing as private and public housing is built. Several of the fine old mansions that once occupied the city are being replaced by apartments, townhouses, or condos. Large brick two-family houses are being built, especially by the growing Portuguese population.

150

The Midtown Merchants Association is seeking to make the center city once more an attractive place to shop. It has prepared maps of the area showing the historic sites, and sponsors regular sidewalk sales to attract people to the stores.

The Eastern Union County Chamber of Commerce has been joined by two other groups: the Elizabeth Chamber of Commerce and the Chamber of Commerce of Union County. Each is promoting the city. All the United Funds in the county have united as one to raise funds for Boy and Girl Scouts and other established agencies in the county.

Where there once were five Lions Clubs there are now only two. One is the new Portuguese Lions Club, which has installed an attractive display on a traffic island on East Grand Street and Elmora Avenue. The other is the Elizabethport Lions Club. The Elizabeth Rotary Club is still functioning.

While the industries that made Elizabeth world famous such as Singers, Phelps Dodge, Simmons, and Bethlehem Steel have moved or closed, numerous small companies have taken their place. Hayward Pool Products, with offices at 900 Fairmount Avenue and several buildings off of Route 1, is the largest with some 1,500 employees. Wakefern Food Corporation at 600 York Avenue supplies food for the Shop-Rite Supermarkets. It is the city's largest employer.

Thomas G. Dunn Jr., superintendent of schools, was cited as the most outstanding superintendent in the state in 2002. He is in charge of a 28-school

Rev. Joseph Garlic, founder and former director of the Elizabethport Presbyterian Center and vice president of Brand New Day, spoke in 1991 in front of a building that was to be renovated by Brand New Day.

Stewart Barney Kean, youngest son of Captain John Kean and Mary Alice Barney Kean, stands in front of the Bonnell House. Kean, who died in May 2002, was president of the Liberty Hall Foundation and an active member of the Elizabethtown Historical Foundation.

program. Two of the schools are former parochial schools that were closed: Holy Rosary School now is Charles J. Hudson School on First Avenue, named for Reverend Father Hudson, who started the Center for Hope Hospice for the terminally-ill in the 1970s. St. Vladimir's School at 425 Grier Avenue is the Terence C. Reilly School, named for a student who was killed in 1989. It originally was operated by St. Vladimir's Ukrainian Catholic Church. It closed about 1986 because asbestos was found in the building. The asbestos was removed and the school sold to the city.

The new Westminster Academy on Westminster Avenue is on the former Janet Memorial Home site, opened in 2000. Unlike the other public schools in the city, the school has open enrollment. Children are selected by a lottery.

Several of the schools have been divided in half to provide classrooms for elementary and middle school pupils. They are the Grover Cleveland Elementary School, now shared with the Mable G. Holmes (the first African-American principal) Middle School on First Avenue, Marquise de Lafayette School and Middle School on Julia Street; and Theodore Roosevelt School and Middle School on Broadway. The Battin High School now is the Christa McAuliffe-Middle School, named for the teacher on the Challenger space shuttle that exploded on January 28, 1986. The Holland School on Bayway Avenue is for gifted and talented fifth and sixth grade students. The William Halloran School 22 has a gifted and talented program for third and fourth graders.

Dr. Thelma C. Hurd, principal of John Marshall School 2 in Elizabethport and an African American, has turned a failing school into one of the top 50 in the nation. All fourth graders passed the language section of the Elementary School Proficiency Assessment test in 2000 and 2001 and 90 percent passed the mathematics section. The children's families are below the poverty level and many of them move frequently. Most of the children qualify for free breakfasts and lunch and need tutorial help. Dr. Hurd expects the teacher to give it. She tells the children that race is no hindrance to achieving their dreams. In September 2002, school officials added 50 children with academic and discipline problems to the school under the city's alternative program.

The school system continues to seek sites for additional buildings. One that is being considered is the land of the Elizabeth Town and Country Club on North Broad Street. Formed in 1894, the club ceased operation of its swimming pool and tennis courts in 2001. A caterer operates the building as "The Old Mansion" for special events only.

Other possible school sites are 3 acres on Trumbull Street, next to Jefferson House of the Elizabeth High School on a lot used as a school warehouse, the vacant Immaculate Conception School on 425 Union Avenue, and the St. Peter and St. Paul Catholic School at 216 Ripley Place. The school board anticipates building an additional high school and several elementary schools.

Three of the parochial schools in Elizabethport have merged as the Elizabethport Catholic School. They are St. Peter and St. Paul Catholic School, a Lithuanian school; St. Adalbert's Parochial School, once Polish, and St. Patrick's Grammar School at 227 Court Street. The Court Street building is being used. St. Patrick's High School and St. Mary of the Assumption grammar school and high school continue to function. Other Catholic schools in Elizabeth are St. Anthony of Padua School at 227 Centre Street, once a large Italian area; Blessed Sacrament School at 1086 North Avenue, once a large Irish section; St. Catherine's at 1003 North Broad Street, once largely Irish; and St. Genevieve's School, 209 Princeton Road, in the Elmora Section.

The city also has two private Roman Catholic Schools: Bender Memorial Academy for children at 416 Linden Avenue and Benedictine Academy at 840 North Broad Street, a private school for girls. Both are operated by Benedictine Sisters of St. Elizabeth. It also has two private Pentecostal schools, the Trinity Christian School at 417 Pennington Street and the Evangel Hispanic School on North Broad Street, originally an Assembly of God Church, which moved to Scotch Plains.

The Jewish Education Center at 330 Elmora Avenue operates schools at the center, the Bruriah High School for Girls, and the Adath Israel School, both on North Avenue. Both buildings were enlarged since 2000. The center also operates Adath Yeshuren Congregation at 200 Murray Street, Elizabeth, and is seeking larger quarters for a facility on Magie Avenue. The center was started by Rabbi Pinchas Teitz in the early 1940s and currently is headed by his son Rabbi Elazar Teitz. The Elmora and Westminster Sections have continued to house a large

153

number of Jewish families. Elizabeth escaped the instances of civil disturbances in Newark and Plainfield in 1967. The people who reside in Elizabeth frequently own and operate businesses in the city limits and enjoy the easy access to them. Several Jewish families in New York City have moved into the section in recent years because they wanted a stable Jewish community within easy commute to New York. The Elmora Hebrew Center at 420 West End Avenue started as a school in 1939. Later it conducted services for the parents of the children. Temple Beth El at 737 North Broad Street, a Reform congregation, disbanded in the 1990s and its congregation united with Sha'arey Shalom Synagogue in Springfield. Only a block away from the Elizabeth line in Hillside, the Conservative Congregation also became orthodox after the immigration of Russian Jews from the former Soviet Union in 1991. A real estate notice on the Internet states that the Westminster Section is a good place for Jewish people to live. Many of the Jewish families have been in the city since the 1880s. The fear that swept through Newark, Plainfield, and Englewood escaped Elizabeth in 1967. Some residents note that the percentage of African Americans has been small compared to the other cities and efforts have been made to integrate the people of the city by official bodies and private organizations.

Temple Israel on East Jersey and Spring Streets closed in 1992, when Rabbi Gershon Chertoff retired. The records of the Conservative temple were sent to Temple Israel in Millburn. Rabbi Chertoff's son Michael served as federal prosecutor in Newark.

Mayor Christian Bollwage discussed his success in attracting new businesses to the city and improving parks and playgrounds in 1993.

The city has a new baseball field with two diamonds on the Elizabeth-Roselle line on Westfield Avenue named Hanratty Field. Another field in Union Township near the Elizabeth line at Morris and North Avenues has been dedicated to Phil Rizzuto of Hillside, the former New York Yankees shortstop and television commentator.

The former Elmora Club at 12 Fernwood Avenue is the Elmora Racquet Club operated by the city's recreation department. It has three tennis courts for youths who wish to play or learn to play. The Fred Exeleben Recreation Center on Richmond Street features a pool and softball field. The Brophy Center on Third Street and the Kenah Center on Fanny Street both have Little League fields. The Arabella Miller Recreation Center on First Street was renamed the Miller Evans Logan Center. A new recreation center was built in 2002-2003.

The city has four passive parks: Jackson, Jefferson, Kellogg, and Carteret; two Union County parks designed by the Olmsted Brothers: Mattano, formerly the Elizabeth River Park; and Warinanco Park on the Roselle line. There also are several small vest-pocket park areas such as Salem Park at the intersection of North Broad Street and Salem Avenue and McPharson at the intersection of Westfield and Elmora Avenues, which are landscaped.

In addition to these, Union County Parks plans to develop park land along the Elizabeth River. In the 1920s, the area along the river was designated as the Elizabeth River Parkway. The river curves too much to place a highway beside it. Several areas along the river have been developed such as the Woodruff Section in Hillside between Conant Street and North Avenue and Mattano Park in Elizabeth.

The City Council in July 2002 issued a bond ordinance for a $2 million senior citizen center next to the Mickey Walker Recreation Center on Anne Street in the Fifth Ward. The center as planned by the Development Concepts of Edison will include a greenhouse, woodworking and pottery room, arts and crafts room, physical exercise classes, and a food pantry and nurse's station.

The Newark Liberty International Airport with some 2,027 acres and the Newark-Elizabeth Seaport with 1,200 acres have reached their potential for expansion. The Port Authority currently is seeking the most effective way to use the land so that services may expand. Nearly half of both the airport and seaport are within Elizabeth's borders.

The 1939 terminal building was moved a mile from its original location and enlarged from its original 14,000 square feet to 100,000 square feet as part of the improvement program for the twenty-first century. The terminal is Building One and is located on Conrad Street named for William "Whitey" Conrad, the airport's first air traffic controller.

Cargo volume at the seaport grew by 5.6 percent in 2001, according to Port Authority Port Commerce Director Richard M. Larrabee. The New York–New Jersey facility saw growth in every sector. All other ports declined, but The Port Authority grew in containerized cargo, bulk, breakbulk, and rail activity. Express Rail, the Port Authority's on-dock rail terminal at the Elizabeth Port Authority Marine Terminal, moved 200,854 containers in 2001 compared to 178,002 in

2000. This was an increase of 12.9 percent. Exports include automobiles, waste paper, plastic products, machinery, and scrap metal.

The Kill Van Kull is being dredged to 45 feet, while Newark Bay or Port Jersey as the Authority calls it is being deepened to 41 feet. New rail and ship-to-rail services are being installed at the Port Newark Container Terminal. The Authority also is seeking to preserve environmentally sensitive tracts of land through the Port Authority's Harbor Restoration Program. Shooter's Island, partially owned by the Cities of Elizabeth and Bayonne and Staten Island, which was used for boat-building in World War I, is now a bird sanctuary.

Elizabeth has come a long way since it was settled in 1664. Through it all Elizabeth has survived and prospered. If John Ogden Sr. could return and see the City of Elizabeth he would be overwhelmed by the changes. Some he would praise and others he would find repugnant. As a man of many parts, he would be fascinated by the changes in buildings such as heating and air conditioning systems, the flow of fresh water from a faucet, and the ability to push a switch and light a room at night.

He would be impressed by the neat houses and lawns on tree-shaded streets and by the flower gardens, but dismayed that few people grow vegetables and fruit to feed themselves. He would be amazed that nearly everyone seemed to own an automobile and that people and material move by motorized vehicles on paved roads. He probably would worry that most people work for somebody else instead of working for themselves.

He would be surprised by the presence of police 24 hours a day, but pleased with their rapid response in emergencies. He would be happy that the bucket brigades were replaced by pumpers to provide water at fires, but would miss the common pasture for cows, sheep, and pigs, and the chicken coops in nearly every yard. He would be pleased with the assortment of foods, furniture, and clothes in the stores, and happy with the presence of hospitals.

Ogden would be amazed by the size of the container ships in the bay and the cargoes they carry to all parts of the world, and by the presence of an airfield, train tracks, and buses to transport people around the city and the nation. He would be fascinated by the moving pictures on television sets and computer screens, but would find his government still coping with being a democracy, his church still worshipping, and the Elizabeth River still flowing to the Arthur Kill. Overall he probably would be pleased with the progress that has been made in the 339 years since he moved to a wilderness and became one of the new town's first Associates. And he would no doubt wonder what could happen next.

BIBLIOGRAPHY

Barber, John W. and Henry Howe. *Historical Collection of New Jersey*. New Haven, CT: John W. Barber, 1868.

Board of Trade of Elizabeth. *Old Home Week*. Elizabeth: 1912.

Clayton, W. Woodford. *History of Union and Middlesex Counties, N.J.* Philadelphia: Everts and Pecks, J.B. Lippincott and Co., 1882.

Cross, Dorothy. *The Indians of New Jersey*. Trenton: Archaeological Society of New Jersey, 1958.

Cunningham, Barbara. *The New Jersey Ethnic Experience*. Union City, NJ: William H. Wise and Co., 1976.

Cunningham, John T. *America's Main Road*. Garden City, NY: Doubleday, 1966.

Drake, J. Madison. *Historical Sketch of the Revolutionary and Civil War*. Elizabeth: Webster Press: 1908.

Ellison, Harry C. *Church of the Founding Fathers of New Jersey*. Corish, ME: Carbrook Press, 1964.

Elizabeth Daily Journal. "City of Elizabeth–Illustrated." Elizabeth: 1889.

Fridlington, Robert J. *Union County Yesterday*. Elizabeth: Union County Cultural and Heritage Programs Advisory Board, 1981.

Gale, Joseph. *Eastern Union: Development of a Jewish Community*. Elizabeth: The Jewish Culture Council of Eastern Union County, 1958.

Hagaman, Adaline. *Early New Jersey*. New York: University Publishing Co., 1964.

Hatfield, Rev. Edwin J. *History of Elizabeth, N.J.* New York: Careton and Lanahan, 1868.

Honeyman, A. Van Doren. *History of Union County, New Jersey, 1664–1923*. Volumes I, II, and III. New York and Chicago: Lewis Publishing Co., 1923.

Kelley, Frank Bergen. "Historic Elizabeth." Elizabeth Sesquicentennial Committee, *Elizabeth Daily Journal*, 1926.

——————. "Historic Elizabeth 1664–1932, George Washington Bicentennial Edition." *Elizabeth Daily Journal*, 1932.

Kennedy, John F. *A Nation of Immigrants*. New York: Harper and Row, 1964.

Kobbe, Gustave. *The Central Railroad of New Jersey*. New York: Central Railroad Co., 1890.

Kraft, Herbert C. *The Lenape Archaeology, History and Ethnography*. Newark: New Jersey Historical Society, 1986.

Lane, Wheaton. *From Indian Trails to Iron Horse*. Princeton University Press, 1939.

Lossing, Benson J. *The Pictorial Field Book of the Revolution*. New York: Harper Brothers, 1850.

Lundin, Leonard. *The Cockpit of the Revolution*. Octagon Books, 1972.

Lyon, A.B. and G.W. *Lyon Memorial: A Genealogy of the Lyon Family*. Detroit: William Graham Co., 1909.

Mayhew, Theodore L. *St. John's Church, Elizabeth, 1706 to 1981, 275th Anniversary*. Elizabeth: St. John's Church, 1981.

McCormick, Richard P. *New Jersey from Colony to State*. Princeton: D. Van Nostrand, 1964.

Mellick, Andrew D. Jr. *The Story of a Old Farm*. New Brunswick, NJ: Rutgers University Press, 1961.

Midtown Elizabeth Directory and Shoppers' Guide. Elizabeth: Midtown Merchants Association, various years.

Murray, Nicholas. *Notes Concerning Elizabethtown*. Elizabeth: E. Saderson, 1844.

Pomfret, John E. *The Providence of East Jersey*. Princeton University Press, 1962.

Ricord, Frederick W. *History of Union County*. Newark: East Jersey History Co., 1897.

Thayer, Theodore. *As We Were: The Story of Old Elizabeth*. Elizabeth: Grassman Publishing Co., 1964.

Turner, Jean-Rae. *Along the Upper Road: History of Hillside, N.J.* Hillside Rotary Club, 1977.

INDEX

www.ingramcontent.com/pod-product-compliance
Lightning Source LLC
Chambersburg PA
CBHW050616110426
42813CB00008B/2574